Teacher's Guide
to the handbook

. . . a teacher's guide to accompany

Write on Track

WRITE SOURCE®

GREAT SOURCE EDUCATION GROUP

a Houghton Mifflin Company
Wilmington, Massachusetts

www.greatsource.com

About the
Teacher's Guide

The *Teacher's Guide* will help you use the *Write on Track* handbook effectively in your classroom, and it will also give you many tips and techniques for working with young writers and learners. We have tried to address the "big questions" teachers are asking today in a way that will help you integrate your professional experience with current research.

If you have any questions, please call. (Use our toll-free number— 1-800-289-4490.) We are always ready to help or receive feedback.

The Write Source/Great Source Education Group

Written and compiled by
Dave Kemper, Ruth Nathan, Patrick Sebranek, and Carol Elsholz
Contributors and consultants: Laura Bachman, Pat Kornelis, Lois Krenzke,
Candyce Norvell, Kelly Brecher Saaf, Lester Smith, Vicki Spandel, Claire Ziffer

Printed in the United States of America

International Standard Book Number: 0-669-48222-6

1 2 3 4 5 6 7 8 9 10 -POO- 07 06 05 04 03 02 01

Table of Contents

A Quick Tour of the Handbook

Write on Track serves as the perfect language handbook for grade 3, one that will help your students improve their ability **to write** (prewriting through publishing), **to think** (creatively, logically, clearly), and **to learn** (in the classroom, in small groups, independently). This quick tour highlights the five main sections of the handbook.

1 The Process of Writing

Students will use this part of the handbook to learn all about the writing process, from choosing a subject to learning about the traits of good writing, from writing with computers to developing paragraphs.

Colorful illustrations and a personal tone make *Write on Track* very attractive to students.

18

Traits of Good Writing

Good writing has interesting ideas, clear organization, personal voice, well-chosen words, smooth sentences, and correct copy. Try using these traits in your writing.

Interesting Ideas ● The writing shares interesting information or ideas.
Clear Organization ● The writing has a beginning, a middle, and an ending.
Personal Voice ●

12

The Writing Process

Writers like Emily use **the writing process**. You should follow the steps in the writing process when you write your own stories, reports, and other things. The writing process will help you do your best work—just like it helps Emily and other writers!

Prewriting

- **Choose** a subject.
- **Gather** details about your subject.
- **Decide** what you want to say about it.

Writing a Draft

- **Write** all of your ideas on paper.
- **Don't** stop to check spelling or punctuation yet.

Helpful checklists, guidelines, and student samples make information easy to use.

13

Revising

- **Read** and review your first draft.
- **Share** your draft with another person.
- **Make** changes to improve your writing.

45

Revising Checklist

✔ **Ideas**
___ Does my writing make sense?
___ Do I need to add any ideas or details?
___ Do I need to cut information that is off the subject?

✔ **Organization**
___ Does my writing have a good beginning?
___ Do I need to move any information to a new place?
___ Does my writing have a good ending?

✔ **Personal Voice**
___ Do I sound like I care about my subject?

✔ **Words and Sentences**
___ Are my words specific and interesting?
___ Are my sentences smooth and easy to read?

---

2 The Forms of Writing

In "The Forms of Writing" section, students will find guidelines and samples for personal narratives, book reviews, news stories, classroom reports, and much more.

80

Making **Albums**

An **album** is a type of scrapbook—a place for special memories. An album may also be a place to collect things. Maybe you collect baseball cards, or stamps, or stickers. If you are interested in anything at all, albums are for you.

Starting Your Album

Some students collect stamps in albums while others collect rare coins. You may even know of someone who has a vacation album. Here is another great idea: You can make an album about your pet or a special person.

126

Writing **Business Letters**

A **business letter** is not like a note or a letter you write to a friend. It is more serious, and it is usually about only one subject. Business letters look alike, too, because they always follow the same form.

Taking Care of Business

Writing business letters can help you in many ways. You can send for things you want, ask for information you need for a project, or even try to solve a problem.

Write on Track addresses forms of personal, subject, workplace, report, and creative writing.

168

Making Friends with a Poem

Once you start writing poems, you will probably enjoy reading them, too. When you read poems, you get to see how they look and hear how they sound. Follow these steps to make friends with each new poem you read.

- **Read the poem to yourself two or three times.**
- **Read it out loud.** (Listen to what it says.)
- **Share the poem with a friend.** (Talk about it.)
- **Copy the poem in a special notebook.**

Now make friends with this poem written by a student like you!

Elephant Poem

Rumbling
    Rumbling
Rumbling
12,000 pounds are coming.
Crashing,
bashing,
    trashing,   mashing,
dashing,   gnashing,
on   leaves.
Elephant noises all around.
            —Claudia Mark

---

3 The Tools of Learning

When students have a question about studying, reading, researching, or thinking, they should turn to this part of the handbook for help.

Reading to Understand

Being a good reader means understanding what you read. And understanding is what reading is all about. It makes reading enjoyable and meaningful. It helps you learn, remember, and discover wonderful things about your world.

Ways to Improve Your Reading

- **Read often.**
- **Read a lot of different things.** (Read information books, newspapers, magazines, and Web sites.)
- **Read at different speeds.** (For example, slow down when there are a lot of facts in the reading.)
- **Use reading strategies to help you understand what you read.** (This chapter will show you how.)

Write on Track **makes all aspects of language and learning active, enjoyable, and meaningful.**

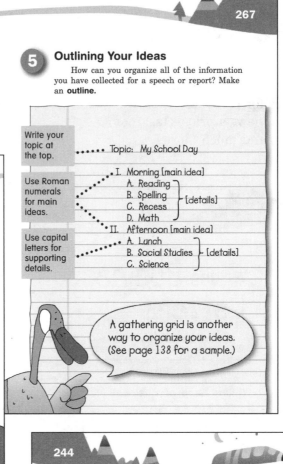

5 Outlining Your Ideas

How can you organize all of the information you have collected for a speech or report? Make an **outline**.

Write your topic at the top. → Topic: My School Day

Use Roman numerals for main ideas. →
I. Morning [main idea]
  A. Reading
  B. Spelling ⎫ [details]
  C. Recess ⎭
  D. Math
II. Afternoon [main idea]

Use capital letters for supporting details. →
  A. Lunch
  B. Social Studies ⎫ [details]
  C. Science ⎭

> A gathering grid is another way to organize your ideas. (See page 138 for a sample.)

Giving Short Talks

Do you and a friend ever sit and talk about a subject you're interested in? Has someone told you how to do something—like fix a flat tire on your bike? Sharing information like that is called conversation. But, when you share the same information with a group, it's called a short talk (or a speech).

Learning by Doing

Giving talks becomes easier with practice. Who knows? You may even start to like it and someday become a famous talker. (Know any famous talkers?) This chapter will help you learn all about giving a short talk—from picking a subject to practicing what you will say.

4 Proofreader's Guide

Whenever students have a question about punctuation, capitalization, usage, and the parts of speech, send them to this color-coded (yellow) section of the handbook.

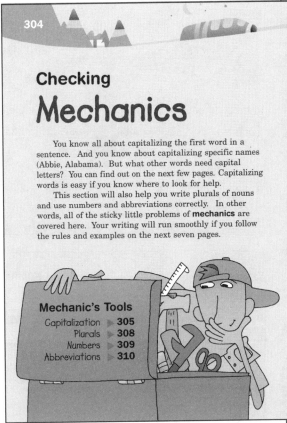

304

Checking
Mechanics

You know all about capitalizing the first word in a sentence. And you know about capitalizing specific names (Abbie, Alabama). But what other words need capital letters? You can find out on the next few pages. Capitalizing words is easy if you know where to look for help.

This section will also help you write plurals of nouns and use numbers and abbreviations correctly. In other words, all of the sticky little problems of **mechanics** are covered here. Your writing will run smoothly if you follow the rules and examples on the next seven pages.

Mechanic's Tools
Capitalization ▶ **305**
Plurals ▶ **308**
Numbers ▶ **309**
Abbreviations ▶ **310**

This easy-to-use guide answers all your students' editing and proofreading questions.

316

Using the
Right Word

This section lists common homophones. Homophones are words that sound the same but have different spellings and meanings, like *to, too,* and *two*. If you know the common homophones, you would write this:

> I blew my nose.
> *not*
> I blue my nose.

ant, aunt	An ant is an insect that works hard. It's a blast when my aunt baby-sits for us.
ate, eight	I ate the teacher's apple. My friend had eight pieces of licorice.
bare, bear	She tested the water with her bare feet. The bear ate the berries.

326

Understanding Our
Language

All the words in our language fit into eight groups. These word groups are called the **parts of speech**.

Nouns **327**
Adverbs **335**
Pronouns **328**
Prepositions **336**
Verbs **329**
Conjunctions **337**
Adjectives **333**
Interjections **337**

6

5 Student Almanac

The last section contains a great deal of helpful information for students to use in all of their classes.

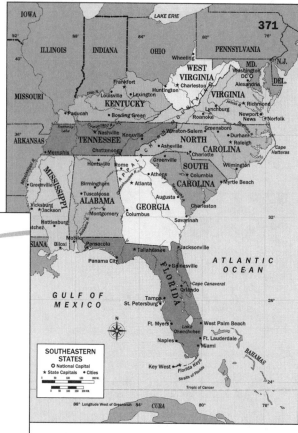

354

Improving
Math Skills

When you think of **math**, what do you think of? Adding numbers? Counting change? Measuring with a ruler? Dividing something into equal parts?

Math is this and much more. Learning math is almost like learning a new language. Math has its own special words and symbols. Math also has its own skills and strategies. This chapter will help you understand the language and strategies of mathematics. At the end of the chapter, you will find all kinds of helpful charts and tables.

Full-color maps, a historical time line, the metric system— *Write on Track* **is truly an all-school handbook.**

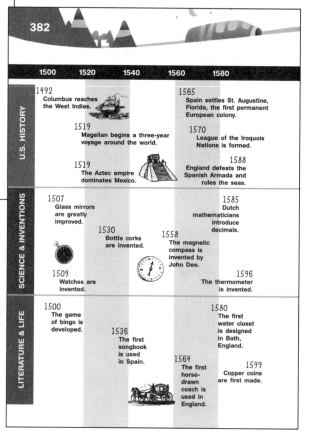

Introducing the Handbook

The pages in this section can be used to introduce *Write on Track* to your students and get them started on the road to becoming active, independent learners.

Getting-Started Activities

We created the *Write on Track* handbook with the goal of making it a handbook students would like and use every day. To make this a reality, students must first understand what's in the handbook and how they can use it. The activities that follow will introduce the handbook to your students and help them become proficient handbook users. (You will find the answer key for the getting-started activities on pages 17-18.)

Scavenger Hunts

Create scavenger hunts asking students to find facts or ideas listed in the handbook. Scavenger hunts can be implemented individually as daily language practice activities or as extended activities, in which you provide students with a series of questions to answer. (See "Reproducible Activities" below for extended activities.)

Example Handbook Scavenger Hunts:

Easy
Turn to page 23. Does the mouse on the page squeak? _*(no)*_

More Challenging
Turn to the index. On what page would you learn how to capitalize days and months? _*(306)*_

A Definite Challenge
On what page would you learn how to bind your own book? _*(55)*_
How many steps does it take? _*six*_

Reproducible Activities

Implement the activity sheets provided for you on pages 10-16. Select only those activities that meet the needs and the nature of your students. Many of the activities can be done by students working in pairs.

Favorite Feature

Give your students the following assignment: Find one page, checklist, chart, illustration, or sample writing in the handbook that you really like or that you think is really important. (Students should be prepared to share their discoveries with a small group of classmates or with the entire class.)

5 W's

Provide small groups of two or three students with *who, what, when, where,* and *why* questions from *Write on Track.* Then have each group find and record answers to these questions. (This activity could be turned into a contest or game.)

Example Questions:

Who writes lists?

What is the last step in the writing process?

Note: A small group of students could develop 5-W's questions for the class to answer.

Wall Charts

Have small groups of students design wall charts based on helpful checklists or guidelines contained in *Write on Track.* (The "Revising Checklist" on page 45 is an example.) Display the finished products in the classroom as well as in other rooms in the school.

Sharing Sessions

Reserve time on Fridays for students to share their positive experiences with the handbook: "I read about the words *to, too,* and *two* in the handbook, and now I know how to use them." Sharing sessions will help students appreciate *Write on Track* as a valuable resource.

Your First Week with the Handbook

Resources: *Write on Track Handbook* (HB), 3, 5-8, 9, 392-400
Write on Track Teacher's Guide (TG), 8-19

Day 1

1. Distribute copies of *Write on Track* and give your students a few minutes to preview the handbook. Have them share first impressions. Then discuss how the handbook is organized, referring students to the introductory page (HB 3), the table of contents (HB 5-8), and the index (HB 392-400).
2. To help students get to know the handbook, ask them to work on one of the reproducible activity sheets. Consider implementing "About the Handbook 1" or "About the Handbook 2" (PG 20-21). *Answer Key* (PG 27)

Day 2

1. Provide time at the beginning of the class period for students to complete their work on the activity sheets. Then discuss the results. *Answer Key* (PG 27)
2. Have students do the "Favorite Feature" activity (PG 18).

Day 3

1. Have students share their points of interest in small groups or with the entire class.
2. Have students do "Complete the Sentences" (PG 22). *Answer Key* (PG 27)

Day 4

1. Read "Why Write?" (HB 9) aloud. Stress the fact that students should keep their handbooks next to them when they write and when they study.
2. With any time remaining, have students work on one of the reproducible activity sheets (PG 23-26). *Answer Keys* (PG 27-28)
3. Consider assigning one of the other getting-started ideas (PG 18).

Day 5

1. Discuss the students' work from the previous day.
2. Have small groups of two or three students develop 5-W's questions (PG 18) that can be used periodically in classroom activities.

Note: Continue reading, sharing, and learning about different parts of the handbook from week to week throughout the school year.

Name

_____

About the Handbook 1

 Turn to the table of contents in your handbook. Write down the page number that would help you answer each question below.

1. How do you write with a *computer*? _____

2. What is *free-verse poetry*? _____

3. What does a *business letter* look like? _____

4. How can you become a *better listener*? _____

5. Why are *punctuation marks* important? _____

 Now turn to the index. Write down a page number that would help you answer each question below.

1. What is an *adjective*? _____

2. How do you write a *cinquain poem*? _____

3. How do you *fold a letter*? _____

4. What is the *plot* of a story? _____

5. Why do you use a *thesaurus*? _____

Name _____

About the Handbook 2

 Turn to the table of contents in your handbook. Write down the page number that would help you answer each question below.

1. What are two ways to *publish* writing? _____

2. When would you write a *summary*? _____

3. How do you write a *photo essay*? _____

4. When is it helpful to *work in groups*? _____

5. How can you improve your *handwriting*? _____

 Now turn to the index. Write down a page number that would help you answer each question below.

1. What do *helping verbs* do? _____

2. When would you use a *Venn diagram*? _____

3. How do you correct a *run-on sentence*? _____

4. What is an *autobiography*? _____

5. When would you use *your* instead of *you're*? _____

Name

_____

Complete the Sentences

 Look through your handbook to find the word or words that complete the following sentences.

1. The name of my handbook is _____.

2. A paragraph that explains something or gives information (page 62)

is called _____ writing.

3. The chapter that begins on page 120 is "_____."

4. One reason to write a business letter (page 127) is to ask for

_____ .

5. One kind of five-line poem (page 175) is _____ .

6. The number one way to improve your reading (page 202) is to

_____ .

7. The suffix that means *without* (page 220) is _____ .

8. Pages in the "Proofreader's Guide" (pages 292-337) are

_____ (color).

9. The first "L" word in the "Checking Your Spelling" list (page 314) is

_____ .

10. In the sentence, "I like hats," the personal pronoun (page 328) is

_____ .

Name _____

Staying on Track

 Look in your handbook to find words from the five different lists named along the top of this chart. Each word must begin with one of the letters in the lefthand column. Two words have been filled in for you.

	Using Prefixes, Suffixes, Roots (pages 216-225)	English from Around the World (page 342)	Using the Right Word (pages 316-321)	Checking Your Spelling (pages 312-315)	State Abbreviations (page 311)
O					
N					
T					
R	rosy				
A					
C					
K	kind				

Name

_____

Handbook Training

> **Answer each question on the monorail trains below.**

1. Name the main sentence in a paragraph.

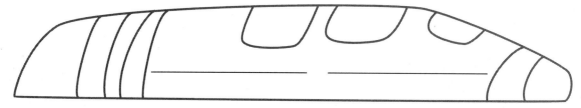

2. List the last step in solving a basic word problem.

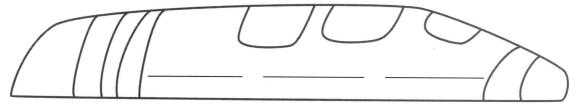

3. Write the first and third steps in the writing process.

4. Name the fairy tale used in the "Writing Plays" chapter.

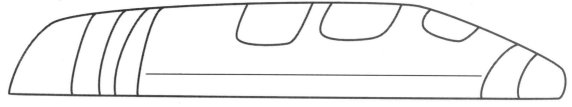

5. List the two basic parts of a sentence.

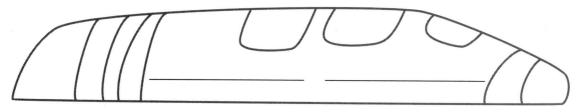

Name _____

Whistle-Stops in *Write on Track*

 Use your handbook to find the information for each stop listed below. The first one has been done for you.

1. *(page 95)* The name of the girl who wrote a friendly letter

A N D R E A

2. *(page 86)* The first food on the list

— — — — — —

3. *(page 229)* The plural of the word *donkey*

— — — — — — —

4. *(page 319)* The homophone for *write*

— — — — — —

5. *(page 103)* Another name for an ABC book

— — — — — — — — — — —

6. *(page 71)* The name of a green vegetable

— — — — — — — —

7. *(page 349)* The name for a female lion

— — — — — — —

8. *(page 389)* The last name of a famous pilot

— — — — — — — — —

9. *(page 158)* The last word on the page

— — —

On Track Write the first letter of each answer. — — — — — — — — —

Unscramble the letters to find a two-word message. *Hint:* It's about getting on a train. — — — — — — — — — — !

Name _____

Write on Track Facts

 Fourteen statements are listed below. Check each statement in the handbook to see if it is true or false. The first one has been done for you.

True   **False**

_____   __X__   **1.** There are 382 pages in *Write on Track*.

_____   _____   **2.** The illustrator of *Write on Track* is Chris Krenzke.

_____   _____   **3.** The table of contents starts on page 4.

_____   _____   **4.** There are three main steps in the writing process.

_____   _____   **5.** A learning log is a wooden book.

_____   _____   **6.** The pages in the "Proofreader's Guide" are yellow.

_____   _____   **7.** A comma is used in numbers of four or more digits.

_____   _____   **8.** A moral is an invented or made-up story.

_____   _____   **9.** KWL is a reading strategy.

_____   _____   **10.** Prefixes are word parts that come at the end of a word.

_____   _____   **11.** Friendly letters and business letters look exactly alike.

_____   _____   **12.** There are two poetry chapters in *Write on Track*.

_____   _____   **13.** The very first date in the historical time line is 1600.

_____   _____   **14.** *Write on Track* has a math chart for skip-counting.

Answer Key

About the Handbook 1

 Turn to the table of contents in your handbook. Write down the page number that would help you answer each question below.

1. How do you write with a *computer*? __22__

2. What is *free-verse poetry*? __167__

3. What does a *business letter* look like? __126__

4. How can you become a *better listener*? __236__

5. Why are *punctuation marks* important? __293__

 Now turn to the index. Write down a page number that would help you answer each question below.

1. What is an *adjective*? __333-334__

2. How do you write a *cinquain poem*? __175__

3. How do you *fold a letter*? __133__

4. What is the *plot of a story*? __119 or 207__

5. Why do you use a *thesaurus*? __214__

10

About the Handbook 2

 Turn to the table of contents in your handbook. Write down the page number that would help you answer each question below.

1. What are two ways to *publish* writing? __52__

2. When would you write a *summary*? __66__

3. How do you write a *photo essay*? __142__

4. When is it helpful to *work in groups*? __280__

5. How can you improve your *handwriting*? __345__

Now turn to the index. Write down a page number that would help you answer each question below.

1. What do *helping verbs* do? __329__

2. When would you use a *Venn diagram*? __266__

3. How do you correct a *run-on sentence*? __73__

4. What is an *autobiography*? __119__

5. When would you use *your* instead of *you're*? __321__

11

Complete the Sentences

 Look through your handbook to find the word or words that complete the following sentences.

1. The name of my handbook is __Write on Track__.

2. A paragraph that explains something or gives information (page 62) is called __expository__ writing.

3. The chapter that begins on page 120 is "__How-To Writing__."

4. One reason to write a business letter (page 127) is to ask for __information__.

5. One kind of five-line poem (page 175) is __cinquain or limerick__.

6. The number one way to improve your reading (page 202) is to __read often__.

7. The suffix that means *without* (page 220) is __less__.

8. Pages in the "Proofreader's Guide" (pages 292-337) are __yellow__ (color).

9. The first "L" word in the "Checking Your Spelling" list (page 314) is __laugh__.

10. In the sentence, "I like hats," the personal pronoun (page 328) is __I__.

12

Staying on Track

 Look in your handbook to find words from the five different lists named along the top of this chart. Each word must begin with one of the letters in the lefthand column. Two words have been filled in for you.

(Answers will vary.)

	Using Prefixes, Suffixes, Roots (pages 216-225)	English from Around the World (page 342)	Using the Right Word (pages 316-321)	Checking Your Spelling (pages 312-315)	State Abbreviations (page 311)
O	octopus	okra	our	ocean	OR
N	negative	night	no	noise	ND
T	telescope	tea	tail	truth	TX
R	rosy	rodeo	read	river	RI
A	astronaut	alphabet	ant	April	AK
C	careless	court	creak	captain	CT
K	kind	ketchup	knight	kitchen	KY

13

Handbook Training

 Answer each question on the monorail trains below.

1. Name the main sentence in a paragraph.

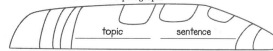
topic   sentence

2. List the last step in solving a basic word problem.

Check   your   answer.

3. Write the first and third steps in the writing process.

prewriting   revising

4. Name the fairy tale used in the "Writing Plays" chapter.

The Three Little Pigs

5. List the two basic parts of a sentence.

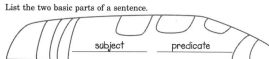
subject   predicate

14

Whistle-Stops in *Write on Track*

 Use your handbook to find the information for each stop listed below. The first one has been done for you.

1. *(page 95)* The name of the girl who wrote a friendly letter

A N D R E A

2. *(page 86)* The first food on the list

A L F A L F A

3. *(page 229)* The plural of the word *donkey*

D O N K E Y S

4. *(page 319)* The homophone for *write*

R I G H T

5. *(page 103)* Another name for an ABC book

A L P H A B E T   B O O K

6. *(page 71)* The name of a green vegetable

B R O C C O L I

7. *(page 349)* The name for a female lion

L I O N E S S

8. *(page 389)* The last name of a famous pilot

L I N D B E R G H

9. *(page 158)* The last word on the page

O U T

On Track > Write the first letter of each answer.

A A D R A B L L O

Unscramble the letters to find a two-word message. *Hint:* It's about getting on a train.

A L L   A B O A R D !

15

Write on Track Facts

 Fourteen statements are listed below. Check each statement in the handbook to see if it is true or false. The first one has been done for you.

True	False	
	X	**1.** There are 382 pages in *Write on Track*.
X		**2.** The illustrator of *Write on Track* is Chris Krenzke.
	X	**3.** The table of contents starts on page 4.
	X	**4.** There are three main steps in the writing process.
	X	**5.** A learning log is a wooden book.
X		**6.** The pages in the "Proofreader's Guide" are yellow.
X		**7.** A comma is used in numbers of four or more digits.
	X	**8.** A moral is an invented or made-up story.
X		**9.** KWL is a reading strategy.
	X	**10.** Prefixes are word parts that come at the end of a word.
	X	**11.** Friendly letters and business letters look exactly alike.
X		**12.** There are two poetry chapters in *Write on Track*.
	X	**13.** The very first date in the historical time line is 1600.
X		**14.** *Write on Track* has a math chart for skip-counting.

16

Minilessons for Using *Write on Track*

 Conduct minilessons on a regular basis to give your students practice using *Write on Track*. Use the samples below as a guide when designing your own minilessons. See pages 206-244 for additional minilessons. Minilessons are activities that can usually be completed in 10-15 minutes.

Bests, Worsts, and Favorites.........Choosing a Subject

■ **MAKE** three columns in your writing notebook.
   WRITE one of these words at the top of each column: *Bests, Worsts, Favorites.*
   LIST writing ideas under each column. (To help you get started, see the top of page 35 in your handbook.)

Wheels of Words...................Using Graphic Organizers

■ **DRAW** a describing wheel on a piece of paper. (See page 265 in your handbook for an example.)
   NAME a favorite object of yours in the middle of the wheel.
   Then **LIST** describing words on the spokes around your subject.
   SHARE your work.

Using the Handbook in the Classroom

Where does *Write on Track* fit in?

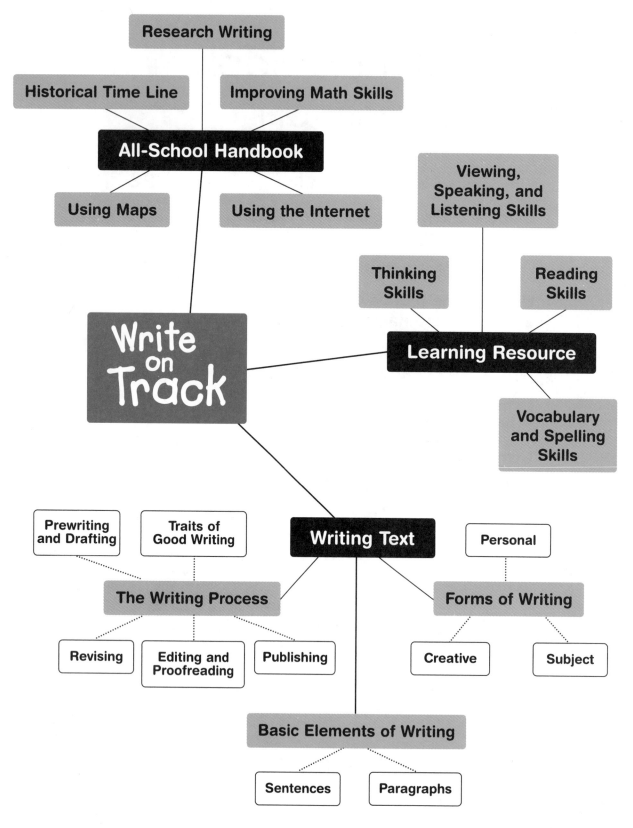

Research Writing

Historical Time Line

Improving Math Skills

All-School Handbook

Using Maps

Using the Internet

Viewing, Speaking, and Listening Skills

Thinking Skills

Reading Skills

Write on Track

Learning Resource

Vocabulary and Spelling Skills

Prewriting and Drafting

Traits of Good Writing

Writing Text

Personal

The Writing Process

Forms of Writing

Revising

Editing and Proofreading

Publishing

Creative

Subject

Basic Elements of Writing

Sentences

Paragraphs

Using the *Write on Track* Handbook in the Language Arts Classroom

Q. **Can teachers develop a language program with *Write on Track* and the *Teacher's Guide*?**

A. Yes. These two resources can serve as the foundation for a language arts program promoting, among other things, student-centered language learning, writing as a process of discovery, and the reading-writing connection. These products can also serve as the foundation for a school-wide writing and learning program.

Because *Write on Track* functions mainly as a writing handbook, that is where teachers should first focus their attention. These are two basic questions that should be answered during initial planning: **How will writing instruction be approached?** Will students engage in writing workshops? Will writing be integrated into thematic units? **What types of writing will be covered?** Will personal forms of writing be emphasized during the first half of the year? Will paragraphs be of primary importance during the second half of the year?

"Effective Writing Instruction," page 158 in this guide, will help teachers answer the first question. Teachers can answer the second question by reviewing the forms of writing covered in the handbook. (Refer to the framework of writing activities listed on page 24 in this guide.)

Q. **What about learning and study skills?**

A. In the "Learning Skills" section (handbook pages 276-291), teachers will find guidelines related to studying and learning. Perhaps writing to learn and note taking could be emphasized during one part of the year, and test taking in the other.

Q. **What about the other language arts?**

A. Teachers will find major sections in the handbook related to searching, thinking, and reading skills.

Finding Information (pages 180-193)
Various primary and secondary sources can be emphasized. In addition, students can begin to explore the Internet and the library in more depth from year to year.

Thinking Skills (pages 262-275)
This section addresses thinking from a number of different perspectives. Graphic organizers help students organize their thinking and writing, from clustering and Venn diagrams to traditional outlining. Problem-solving skills help students distinguish between facts and opinions. There are also tips for keeping learning logs.

Reading and Spelling Skills (pages 194-229)
We suggest that the glossary of prefixes, suffixes, and roots should be a tool of vocabulary study. (See pages 216-225 in the handbook.)

Q. **What else should teachers remember when planning with *Write on Track*?**

A. Teachers should always remember to turn to the "Introductory Notes" in this teacher's guide (pages 33-156) whenever they are planning a unit around a particular chapter in the handbook.

Overview of the Writing Units

SENTENCES AND PARAGRAPHS	
Writing Sentences	Writing Basic Sentences Combining Sentences
Writing Paragraphs	Writing Paragraphs (Four Types) Writing a Summary

PERSONAL WRITING	
Writing in Journals	Journal Writing
Writing Personal Narratives	Personal Narrative
Writing Notes and Letters	Friendly Notes and E-Mail Friendly Letter

SUBJECT WRITING	
Writing Family Stories	Family Story
Writing News Stories	Newspaper Story Human-Interest Story
Writing Book Reviews	Fiction Book Review Nonfiction Book Review
How-To Writing	Explanation Directions
Writing Business Letters	Letter Asking for Information Letter to Solve a Problem

STORY, PLAY, AND POETRY WRITING	
Writing Stories	Realistic Story Time-Travel Fantasy
Writing Plays	Playwriting
Writing Poems	Free-Verse Poetry Traditional and Playful Poetry

REPORT WRITING	
Making an Album	Album Making
Writing Classroom Reports	Classroom Report
Writing Photo Essays	Photo Essay

How are the modes of writing covered in the handbook?

Many language arts curriculums approach writing according to the different modes of writing: narrative, descriptive, expository, and persuasive. The chart below shows how the modes of writing are covered in the *Write on Track* handbook. You may find this chart helpful when planning writing assignments.

Narrative

Narrative Paragraph, **60**

Writing in a Personal Journal, **78**

Making Albums, **80-81**

Writing Personal Narratives, **82-85**

Writing Friendly Notes, **90-93**

Writing Friendly Letters, **94-97**

Writing Family Stories, **98-101**

Human-Interest Story, **112**

Writing Realistic Stories, **149-153**

Writing Time-Travel Fantasies, **154-159**

Writing Plays, **160-165**

Descriptive

Descriptive Paragraph, **61**

Writing Book Reviews, **114-118**

How-To Writing, **120-125**

Writing Free-Verse Poetry, **167-173**

Traditional and Playful Poetry, **174-179**

Expository

Expository Paragraph, **62**

Writing a Summary, **66-69**

Writing in a Reading Journal, **79**

Writing Lists, **86-89**

Writing Alphabet Books, **103-107**

Writing Newspaper Stories, **108-111**

Writing Business Letters, **126-133**

Writing Classroom Reports, **135-141**

Writing Photo Essays, **142-147**

Giving Short Talks, **244-249**

Persuasive

Persuasive Paragraph, **63**

Writing a Letter to the Editor, **113**

Writing a Business Letter—To Solve a Problem, **132**

Using the Handbook as an All-School Writing and Learning Guide

Because there is such a wide range of information covered in *Write on Track*, it can be used in many different ways. For example, in many schools the handbook serves as an **all-school resource**—one that students refer to during every class for help with their writing, study-reading, note taking, test taking, and so on. Once teachers become familiar with the contents of the handbook, they will understand its potential as a writing and learning tool.

Special Note: See "Writing Throughout the Day" on pages 167-170 in this guide for more information about writing in the subject areas.

Writing Skills

- Why Write? (9)
- Steps in the Writing Process (12-13)
- Writing with a Computer (22-27)
- Gathering Details (36-37)
- Writing Paragraphs (56-65)
- Expository Writing (62)
- Persuasive Writing (63)
- Writing Business Letters (126-133)
- Thinking Clearly (268-273)
- Writing to Learn (274-275)

Researching Skills

- Writing a Summary (66-69)
- Writing Classroom Reports (135-141)
- Using the Library (181-187)
- Using the Internet (188-193)
- Multimedia Computer Reports (250-251)

Reading Skills

- Reading Graphics (195-199)
- Reading New Words (200-201)
- Reading to Understand (202-207)
- Building Vocabulary Skills (209-215)

Viewing, Speaking, and Listening Skills

- Learning to View (231-235)
- Learning to Listen (236-237)
- Performing Poems (238-243)
- Giving Short Talks (244-251)
- Telling Stories (256-261)

Study Skills

- Completing Assignments (277-279)
- Working in Groups (280-283)
- Taking Tests (284-291)

Helpful Charts and Lists

- The Metric System (352-353)
- Math Symbols, Numbers, and Tables (359-362)
- Maps (367-376)
- Historical Time Line (382-391)

Using the Handbook for Standards-Based Instruction

Today, teachers are expected to use standards to inform instruction. Standards are the tools used to justify and document what is being taught and what students are achieving. As you will see on the next four pages, *Write on Track* can serve as an important resource for planning instruction that meets the essential *writing standards* as developed at the national, state, and/or local level. (The performance standards that follow reflect the writing skills and forms that students should understand and employ by grade 3.)

The Process of Writing

Understanding How Writing Works

The student is expected to . . .	Handbook Pages
• **use** prewriting strategies such as graphic organizers, drawings, and lists to generate ideas.	33-35, 263-267
• **write** in different forms for different purposes.	77-179
• **focus** on a central idea.	36-37
• **write** drafts with a consideration for audience and purpose.	37, 38-39
• **use** anecdotes, descriptions, and vivid language to support ideas.	18-21, 43-44, 153, 173
• **revise** selected drafts by adding, rearranging, deleting, and improving text—striving for better word choice and consistency.	16, 41-45, 46-48
• **edit** drafts for features of polished writing such as appropriate grammar, spelling, capitalization, and punctuation.	50-51
• **use** available technology to support aspects of creating, drafting, revising, editing, and publishing texts.	22-27, 188-193, 250-251

Evaluating Written Work

The student is expected to . . .	Handbook Pages
• **assess** writing according to the traits of good writing.	18-21
• **respond** in constructive ways to others' writing.	46-48
• **use** published examples as models for writing.	18-21
• **review** a collection of his or her own writing to monitor growth as a writer.	28-30

The Forms of Writing

Writing to Share

The student is expected to develop . . .   Handbook Pages

- **paragraphs** (narrative, descriptive, expository, persuasive) that . . .   **57-65**
  - contain three or more sentences about the same subject.
  - develop a topic sentence and related closing sentence.
  - include simple supporting facts and details.

- **narratives** that . . .   **82-85, 98-101,**
  - recount in sequence several parts of a personal experience or   **149-153, 154-159**
    fictitious tale.
  - use details (some sensory) that develop the plot of the story.

- **news stories** that . . .   **108-113**
  - contain a lead and byline.
  - contain a beginning, a well-developed middle, and an ending.

- **friendly and business letters** that . . .   **94-97, 126-133**
  - consider audience, purpose, and context.
  - include all parts of a letter.

- **directions** that . . .   **120-125**
  - identify the sequence of steps needed to do something or to get
    somewhere.

- **classroom reports** that . . .   **135-141, 142-147**
  - contain a beginning that introduces the subject.
  - contain a middle that answers questions about the subject.
  - contain an ending that concludes with an important idea about
    the subject.

- **poems** that . . .   **167-173, 174-179**
  - reflect an awareness of pleasing sounds of language.
  - express feelings and/or capture sights and sounds in words.

- **summaries** that . . .   **66-69**
  - contain the most important details from a reading.

- **responses to literature** that . . .   **114-119**
  - demonstrate an understanding of a literary work.
  - support judgments through references to the text or to personal
    knowledge.

Writing to Learn

The student is expected to . . .   Handbook Pages

• **write** to express, discover, record, develop, reflect on, and refine ideas.	**80-81, 90-93, 274-275**
• **create** learning logs, daily journal entries, and lists as tools for learning in all subjects.	**77-79, 86-89, 103-107, 274-275, 277-279, 282-283**

The Mechanics of Writing

Research

The student is expected to . . .   Handbook Pages

• **collect** information about a topic.	**36-37, 136-138, 181-186, 191-192**
• **construct** questions about a topic.	**136-138**
• **record** his or her own knowledge of a topic in a variety of ways, such as by drawing pictures, making lists, keeping a learning log, and showing connections among ideas.	**33-35, 36-37, 86-89, 103-107**
• **take** simple notes from relevant sources, such as guest speakers, books, encyclopedias, interviews, and media sources.	**211, 237**
• **use** print and electronic sources to locate books.	**181-186**
• **understand** and be able to use table of contents, chapter and selection headings, glossary, and index to locate information in a reference book.	**187**
• **understand** the appropriate use and structure of various reference materials, such as dictionary, thesaurus, and encyclopedia.	**186, 191, 212-214**
• **present** information in various forms using available technology.	**188-193**

Grammar and Usage

The student is expected to . . .   Handbook Pages

- **apply** standard English grammar and usage, including   **72, 322-324**
  subject-verb agreement and appropriate verb tenses, with
  increasing accuracy to communicate clearly and effectively
  in writing.

- **understand** and be able to use complete and correct sentences   **21, 72-73,**
  of varying length.   **325**

- **eliminate** sentence fragments, run-on sentences, and rambling   **73**
  sentences with increasing accuracy.

- **identify** and correctly use the parts of speech.   **326-337**

- **correctly** use common compound words, contractions,   **201, 299,**
  and homophones.   **316-321**

Punctuation, Capitalization, and Spelling

The student is expected to . . .   Handbook Pages

- **punctuate** with increasing accuracy.   **293-303**

- **capitalize** titles, proper nouns, and sentences correctly.   **305-307**

- **use** regular and irregular plurals correctly.   **308**

- **spell** roots, prefixes, and suffixes, compound words, contractions,   **215, 216-225**
  and syllable constructions correctly.

- **write** with more proficient spelling of regularly spelled patterns   **226-229, 312-315,**
  and homophones.   **316-321**

- **use** resources such as dictionaries to find correct spellings,   **212-214**
  synonyms, and replacement words.

- **gain** awareness of the influence of other languages and   **339-343**
  cultures on the spelling of English words.

Using *Write on Track* to Meet the Needs of Every Student

Teachers can't possibly accommodate all of their students' different learning styles following a standard text, one chapter after another. What works best is a language resource like *Write on Track*, providing useful information and guidelines that each student can turn to on his or her own terms.

Students refer to *Write on Track* when they need information—in any class, at any time. We like to call *Write on Track* a contextbook because students use it, in context, as they develop a piece of writing, study for a test, prepare for an interview, and so on. *Write on Track,* more than a textbook can, evokes student-directed learning. It accommodates the different learning needs of all students.

1 Reform and Restructuring

We strongly believe that the primary role of instruction should be to help students improve their emerging learning abilities and explore their own interests. Instead of the assembly-line approach to teaching, with homogeneous students as the end product, students should be met on their own terms, with their individual needs at the core of the curriculum. For educators to do this, they must change their approach: Whether each learner is progressing must be the main concern, not the level of content covered.

2 Student-Centered Learning

Certainly this method of instruction makes the most sense in language arts instruction since no two students progress as writers and readers at the same speed or in the same way. To make instruction more student centered, many language arts teachers run their classrooms as writing and reading workshops. In workshops, students write at their own pace, read books that interest them, interact, take risks, decide what projects to work on next, and so on.

We've used the workshop approach in our own classrooms, so we know how effective it can be. Former students tell us all the time how they really learned to write and read in our language arts classes. It's also because of the workshop approach that we developed our first handbook. We did it to give our students a basic resource they could refer to when writing and learning.

3 Meeting Everyone's Needs

Once your students have their own copies of *Write on Track*, we can't urge you enough to turn your classroom into a workshop. It is the best way to meet your students' individual needs. Everyone reads, writes, and learns together. When workshops are used effectively, large-scale grouping or tracking isn't necessary.

4 Making It Work

Workshop teachers must become effective managers of their classrooms, providing an atmosphere conducive to writing and learning. They must guide students during personal conferences and editing sessions, and in occasional whole-class instruction, toward a mastery of basic skills.

Using the Handbook with the Complete *Write on Track* Program

The *Write on Track* handbook works by itself as an extremely effective writing and learning guide and can be used for a number of different purposes—many of which are discussed on the previous pages in this section of your *Teacher's Guide*.

The handbook also serves as the core resource for the **Write on Track Language Program.** (See below for more information.)

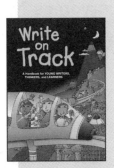

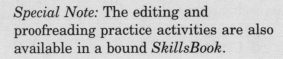

Working with the Program

Students refer to the *Write on Track* handbook to help them complete their work in the program.

Teachers refer to the *Teacher's Guide* (this guide) for basic planning ideas, start-up activities, and minilessons.

Teachers who purchase the complete program receive a *Program Guide* ring binder, providing teaching units for each chapter in the handbook (introductory notes, daily lesson plans, blackline masters, and minilessons), editing and proofreading practice activities, and much more. All program guide activities are reproducible.

Special Note: The editing and proofreading practice activities are also available in a bound *SkillsBook*.

The Process of Writing

Introductory Notes

This section introduces "The Process of Writing" chapters in the handbook and provides getting-started ideas to help you with your initial planning.

All About Writing

(See handbook pages 11-13.)

In her book, *Living Between the Lines*, Lucy McCormick Calkins states, "The reason so many of us care so much about the teaching of reading and writing is that when we give the children the words they need, we are giving them life and growth, and refreshment." Her words provide a perfect introduction to *Write on Track*. We believe that the information in "The Process of Writing" gives students the words they need to live and grow as young writers.

Rationale
- Writing helps students learn about themselves and the world around them.
- Writing is a process of developing and exploring more than it is an end product.
- The writing process provides students with a basic framework, or blueprint, helping them learn and grow as writers.

Major Concepts
- **Writing is many different things, including a satisfying way to share and to learn.** (page 11)
- **The process of writing involves prewriting, drafting, revising, editing and proofreading, and publishing.** (pages 12-13)

Performance Standards - - - -
Students are expected to . . .
- approach writing as a process.

Getting Started with "All About Writing"

Start-Up Activity: Ask students to share some of their successes with writing activities. Invite them to bring in something they wrote last year to share with the class. Then discuss this quotation by Jane Yolen: "It's never perfect when I write it the first time, or the second time, or the fifth time. But it always gets better as I go over it and over it."

Enrichment Activity: Engage students in making a classroom bulletin board related to the writing process. They may add to it and modify it throughout the year.

Teaching Resources

Write on Track Teacher's Guide

- Minilessons:

    "There's nothing I like better . . . !" (page 206)

    "Following the Dotted Line" (page 206)

Write on Track Handbook

- "Why Write?" page 9, discusses important reasons for writing.
- "One Writer's Process," pages 14-17, leads students through the steps one writer uses to develop a personal narrative using the writing process.
- "Prewriting and Drafting Guide," pages 32-39, and "Revising and Editing Guide," pages 40-55, give guidelines for each step in the writing process.

Write on Track Program Guide

- A teaching unit (lesson plans, blackline masters, and additional minilessons) can be found in the Program Guide ring binder.

One Writer's Process

(See handbook pages 14-17.)

Most young writers, especially if they are new to the writing process, may not appreciate that writing must go through a series of changes before it becomes effective. Once they get all of their ideas on paper, they feel that their writing is essentially complete, except for making a few surface changes. As you know, and as your students will learn, one draft is not enough. Real writing, writing that speaks clearly and completely, results from drafting and careful revising and editing.

Rationale
- Seeing the writing process in action helps students understand how it works.
- The writing process is a series of choices a writer makes as she or he develops an idea.

Major Concepts
- **Prewriting involves selecting a subject and collecting details.** (page 14)
- **A first draft is a first look at a developing writing idea.** (page 15)
- **Revising means making improvements in a piece of writing.** (page 16)
- **Editing and proofreading involves checking for errors in usage, punctuation, grammar, and spelling.** (page 16)

Performance Standards

Students are expected to . . .
- approach writing as a process to help them do their best writing work.
- use prewriting strategies, such as graphic organizers, drawings, and lists, to generate ideas.
- write drafts with a consideration for audience and purpose.
- revise selected drafts by changing, moving, and adding text.
- edit and proofread drafts for correct copy.

Getting Started with "One Writer's Process"

Start-Up Activity: Ask students to answer the following questions about their own writing:
1. What are some things I would like to write about?
2. Do I think writing is easy or hard? Explain.
3. What are some things that good writers do?
4. If part of my writing doesn't make sense, what can I do about it?
5. How can I check for errors in my writing?

Enrichment Activity: Have students relate the steps of the writing process to something they have written or to a piece of student writing you project on an overhead.

Teaching Resources

Write on Track Teacher's Guide
- Minilessons:

  "My Day at the Derby" (page 206)

  "By Peter" (page 207)

Write on Track Handbook
- The writing process is further developed by "Prewriting and Drafting Guide," pages 32-39, and "Revising and Editing Guide," pages 40-55.

Write on Track Program Guide
- A teaching unit (lesson plans, blackline masters, and additional minilessons) can be found in the Program Guide ring binder.

Traits of Good Writing

- Interesting Ideas
- Clear Organization
- Personal Voice
- Well-Chosen Words
- Smooth Sentences
- Correct Copy

(See handbook pages 18-21.)

The traits of good writing are like the road signs of writing. Road signs help drivers know speed limits, locate exits and rest areas, and learn of road hazards or problems. The traits of good writing help students make their writing interesting and well organized, use colorful and inviting language, and avoid errors in final copy.

Rationale
- Teaching about the traits of good writing and pointing them out in children's literature will help students use these traits in their own writing.
- Working with the traits of good writing during writing and revising can help all writers improve and enrich their writing skills.

Major Concepts
- **The traits of good writing can be identified and defined.** (pages 18-21)
- **Good literature models the traits of good writing.** (pages 18-21)

Performance Standards

Students are expected to . . .
- assess writing according to standards.
- use published examples as models for writing.

Getting Started with "Traits of Good Writing"

Start-Up Activity: List the traits of good writing on the chalkboard. Then have all students turn to a page or section from something the class is reading. After you have done the reading, ask students to identify specific parts of the section that demonstrate certain traits.

Enrichment Activity: Create scrapbooks with a section for each of the traits of good writing. As students are reading independently, have them copy writing they find in books, in newspapers, or on the Internet that demonstrates a specific trait. Add each example to the scrapbook. This activity can be done by individuals, small groups, or the whole class.

Teaching Resources

Write on Track Teacher's Guide

- Minilessons:

    "From Top to Bottom" (page 207)

    "Computer Personality" (page 207)

- "The Trait-Based Approach" (pages 164-165)
- "Assessment Strategies and Rubrics" (pages 171-180)

Write on Track Handbook

- "Revising Checklist," page 45, addresses several of the traits of good writing.

Write on Track Program Guide

- A teaching unit (lesson plans, blackline masters, and additional minilessons) can be found in the Program Guide ring binder.

Writing with a Computer

(See handbook pages 22-27.)

Students are generally enthusiastic about working with a computer. As teachers, we must share in this enthusiasm and appreciate how word-processing programs, multimedia programs, and drawing programs have enhanced students' writing skills. To do otherwise would be to ignore some very encouraging research about computer-assisted writing: Computers help students stay with a piece of writing longer. They make revising more accessible, promote collaboration, build self-esteem, and so on.

Rationale
- The personal computer is an important writing and learning tool.
- Computers facilitate writing as a process.

Major Concepts
- **The computer can be a writer's best friend.** (page 22)
- **It's important to know the basic parts of a personal computer.** (page 23)
- **It's important to understand how to use a computer as a writing tool.** (page 24)
- **Writing with a computer requires learning to use the keyboard.** (pages 25-27)

Performance Standards

Students are expected to . . .
- use available technology to support aspects of creating, revising, editing, and publishing texts.
- present information in various forms using available technology.

Getting Started with "Writing with a Computer"

Start-Up Activity: Discuss these two questions with the students. What could you teach someone else to do on a computer? What would you like to learn to do on a computer?

Enrichment Activity: Create a Venn diagram (handbook page 266) on a chart or chalkboard, comparing and contrasting writing with a pencil and writing with a word-processing program. Ask student volunteers to give brief oral reports, using the Venn diagrams as their graphic support.

Teaching Resources

Write on Track Teacher's Guide

*   Minilessons:

    "Getting to Know PC" (page 207)

    "The Name Game" (page 208)

Write on Track Handbook

*   "Computer Keyboard," pages 26-27, gives students a place to practice keyboarding and shows the proper placement of fingers on the keyboard.

*   "Using the Internet," pages 188-193, presents more information about using computers in the classroom.

Write on Track Program Guide

*   A teaching unit (lesson plans, blackline masters, and additional minilessons) can be found in the Program Guide ring binder.

Planning Portfolios

(See handbook pages 28-31.)

"Planning Portfolios" introduces students to two types of portfolios: personal and classroom. A *personal portfolio* is a place for students to collect their writing for their own use. A *classroom portfolio* is a place for students to showcase their best and favorite writings in school.

Rationale
- Planning and compiling portfolios provide students with excellent opportunities to learn and to grow as writers.
- Classroom portfolios provide an authentic means of assessment.
- Portfolios encourage students to reflect upon their writing.

Major Concepts
- **A portfolio is a special collection of an individual's writing.** (page 28)
- **A personal portfolio can be set up in different ways.** (page 29)
- **A classroom portfolio includes writing examples plus evaluation sheets.** (page 30)
- **Developing an effective classroom portfolio requires careful planning and organizing.** (page 31)

Performance Standards - - - - -

Students are expected to . . .
- review a collection of their work to determine strengths and weaknesses.

Getting Started with "Planning Portfolios"

Start-Up Activity: Ask students to briefly tell what, if anything, they collect. Compare a portfolio to a personal collection of special objects. Explain the difference between a showcase portfolio (a keepsake of special writings), a growth portfolio (a collection of writings to show improvement), and a writing folder (a place where all writing and writing ideas are kept).

Enrichment Activity: Encourage students to keep personal portfolios as explained on page 29 in the handbook.

Teaching Resources

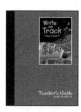

Write on Track Teacher's Guide
- Minilessons:

  "Title Time" (page 208)

  "Saving the Best" (page 208)
- "Assessment Strategies and Rubrics" (pages 171-180)

Write on Track Handbook
- "Response Sheet," page 49, helps students get reactions to their writing from classmates.

Write on Track Program Guide
- A teaching unit (lesson plans, blackline masters, and additional minilessons) can be found in the Program Guide ring binder.

Choosing a Subject

(See handbook pages 33-35.)

Professional writers are constantly making observations and absorbing ideas they can use in their stories and essays. Here's what Steven Kellogg, a well-known writer and illustrator, says about the writer's life: "I'm always storing up images and expressions in my memory file that I can flip through and draw upon when I'm actually working." If students take the time to look, listen, and learn, they will also find plenty of interesting things to write about.

Rationale	• Writers are always collecting ideas for their work.
	• Writing is more than putting words on paper. It is reading, observing, listening, and reflecting.
	• Writing becomes rewarding when it stems from a writer's interests and concerns.

Major Concepts	• **It's important to keep track of good writing ideas in a notebook.** (pages 33-34)
	• **Students can build a file of writing ideas to choose from when they want to write.** (pages 34-35)

Performance Standards - - - - -

Students are expected to . . .
- use prewriting strategies, such as graphic organizers, drawings, and lists, to generate ideas.

Getting Started with "Choosing a Subject"

Start-Up Activity: Beginning with this unit, encourage each student to keep an ongoing writer's notebook. Have students set up their notebooks in three parts: (1) Things I see and hear; (2) Best, Worst, and Favorite Events; (3) Ideas from books. (Sometimes small-sized notebooks are more accessible than larger ones for jotting notes about things that happen.)

Enrichment Activity: Have students create their own life maps. Encourage them to use the map on page 34 in the handbook as a model.

Teaching Resources

Write on Track Teacher's Guide

- Minilessons:

  "Good News, Bad News" (page 208)

  "The Road of Life" (page 208)

Write on Track Handbook

- "Gathering Details," pages 36-37 and "Writing a First Draft," pages 38-39, continue the discussion on prewriting activities.

Write on Track Program Guide

- A teaching unit (lesson plans, blackline masters, and additional minilessons) can be found in the Program Guide ring binder.

Gathering Details

(See handbook pages 36-37.)

Information empowers students; it provides them with incentive to write because they have knowledge to share. Information gathering is especially important for students in grades three through six as they begin to write reports and essays. Teachers in these grades have the important task of helping students become skilled information gatherers.

Rationale
- Learning how to learn (how to acquire knowledge) should be an integral part of a writing program.
- Collecting details is an important aspect of prewriting.
- Students must be given opportunities to pursue some topics in depth.

Major Concepts
- **Details are the facts and ideas that make writing interesting.** (page 36)
- **Collecting details includes researching, talking, and brainstorming.** (pages 36-37)
- **Listing, answering the 5 W's, and clustering are effective ways to collect ideas.** (page 37)
- **Before writing a first draft, writers should be able to identify their subject, purpose, form, and audience.** (page 37)

Performance Standards

Students are expected to . . .
- use prewriting strategies, such as graphic organizers, drawings, and lists, to generate ideas.
- focus on a central idea.
- organize the information they have gathered.

Getting Started with "Gathering Details"

Start-Up Activity: Ask one or two students to tell you about an interesting or unusual experience they have had recently. Then write the 5 W's—Who? What? When? Where? Why?—on the chalkboard and ask students to write about an interesting or unusual time, using the 5 W's. (Discuss how using the 5 W's as a gathering tool made it easier to do this writing.)

Enrichment Activity: To add a dimension of reality to students' writing, have them learn how to conduct interviews. See pages 252-255 in the handbook for detailed instructions on what to do before, during, and after an interview.

Teaching Resources

Write on Track Teacher's Guide
- Minilessons:
  "5 × W = 5 W's" (page 209)
  "Point by Point" (page 209)

Write on Track Handbook
- "Choosing a Subject," pages 33-35, acts as a lead-in to this chapter.
- "Using Graphic Organizers," pages 263-267, shows several helpful ways to gather details.

Write on Track Program Guide
- A teaching unit (lesson plans, blackline masters, and additional minilessons) can be found in the Program Guide ring binder.

Writing a First Draft

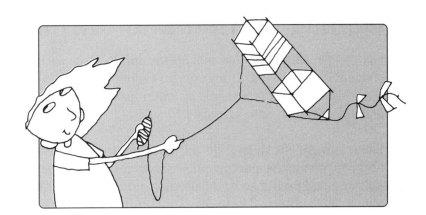

(See handbook pages 38-39.)

Many experienced writers practice their craft because they feel a need to create and explore. It's in their bones. Some young writers feel the same way. They like nothing better than inventing stories and poems, dashing off notes, and writing about their experiences. You may be fortunate enough to have a few of these writers in your classroom. Give them time and freedom and let them go to work. Your challenge is to so engage students that writing becomes part of them—they'll feel it in their bones.

Your job will be easier if you establish a writer-friendly classroom based on the following principles:

1. Writing is a process more than it is an end product.
2. Young writers should write about subjects that interest them.
3. They should share their work throughout the writing process.
4. They should write with sincere and genuine feelings.
5. They should write for real readers.

Rationale
- A first draft is a writer's early look at an emerging writing idea.
- The beginning of a piece of writing should grab the readers' attention.
- The middle part of a draft should explain the details related to the main idea.
- The ending of a draft should relate back to the main idea.

Major Concepts
- **It is important to pay special attention to the beginning part of a draft.** (page 38)
- **The purpose of a first draft is not to write a perfect paper, but to get all of the ideas on paper.** (page 39)

Performance Standards

Students are expected to . . .
- focus on a central idea.
- write drafts with consideration for audience and purpose.

Getting Started with "Writing a First Draft"

Start-Up Activity: Ask each student to find an effective beginning in a favorite book to share with the class. Students can review the writing models in the handbook or consider the stories in classroom readers or trade books. Write some sample beginnings on the board and discuss why they are effective.

Enrichment Activity: Do an "oral paragraph" about something you are studying in class. You can begin the paragraph with an interesting sentence—either a question or an unusual statement. For the middle, have a number of students explain or describe important details about the subject. Then, for the ending, have someone make up a sentence, summarizing what has been offered. Point out how the creation of this roughly gathered "paragraph" is like writing a first draft.

Teaching Resources

Write on Track Teacher's Guide

- Minilessons:

  "Starting with a Bang" (page 209)

  "The Most Exciting . . . " (page 209)

Write on Track Handbook

- "Gathering Details," pages 36-37, especially the questions about *subject, purpose, form, audience,* and *voice,* helps students find direction for their first drafts and organize their details.

- "The Basic Parts of a Paragraph," page 58, "A Closer Look at the Parts," page 59, and "Checking Your Organization," page 43, offer additional examples of organizing details in a first draft.

Write on Track Program Guide

- A teaching unit (lesson plans, blackline masters, and additional minilessons) can be found in the Program Guide ring binder.

Revising Your Writing

(See handbook pages 41-45.)

Writers improve upon what they have written by rereading their work and rewriting the parts that need to be changed. This process is called revision. Among other things, writers read and listen for meaning, voice, and organization. Revision is important for all writers, not only because it provides an opportunity to make a draft better, but also because it frees the writer to take risks during the drafting process.

Rationale
- Many students think that good writers sit down and write finished, polished pieces the first time through. This rarely happens.
- When young writers see that time away from their drafts helps them find its strong and weak points, they feel better about taking risks earlier in the writing process.
- Knowing how the revision process works can help writers understand how good writing gets done.

Major Concepts
- **Writing can be changed to make it better.** (page 41)
- **It helps to read a draft aloud and then put it aside for awhile.** (page 42)
- **Beginnings need to interest readers and name the subject.** (page 43)
- **The middle of a draft adds details and explores the subject.** (page 43)
- **Endings should be interesting and remind the readers about the subject.** (page 43)
- **Writers can learn to "show, don't tell."** (page 44)

Performance Standards

Students are expected to . . .
- revise selected drafts by adding and rearranging text, deleting text that is off the subject, and improving sequence—striving for increased detail, clarity, correct order of ideas, and better word choice.

Getting Started with "Revising Your Writing"

Start-Up Activity: Invite a slightly older student into your class to talk about the revising process. You might ask the student to bring in drafts of a finished piece and to discuss how he or she worked on it. Your students could conduct an interview with this writer. (See "Learning to Interview" on pages 252-255 in the handbook.)

Enrichment Activity: Sometimes young writers give the whole story away in the first line: "Last year our class guinea pig had 12 babies." Challenge students to write several sentences that would lead up to the "12 babies" as a surprise ending. Here's one way to save the surprise until the end: "No one thought much of our guinea pig last year. She was so quiet. She sat around all day doing nothing. Every once in a while she got up to eat. But one day . . . "

Teaching Resources

Write on Track Teacher's Guide

- Minilessons:

  "Off the Subject" (page 210)

  "Show Me!" (page 210)

Write on Track Handbook

- "Traits of Good Writing," pages 18-21, covers helpful revising information.

- "Working with Partners," pages 46-49, offers a response sheet and advice to help students take revising suggestions from classmates.

Write on Track Program Guide

- A teaching unit (lesson plans, blackline masters, and additional minilessons) can be found in the Program Guide ring binder.

Working with Partners

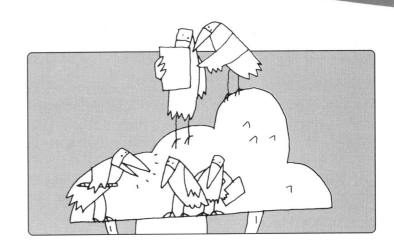

(See handbook pages 46-49.)

When children talk about their writing to others, they are holding a conference. The process of conferring with partners often gives writers insights, which in turn help them gain control over their writing process. Conferences can be done with one partner or in small groups of three or four students.

Rationale
- As writers review their own writing, they try to look at it with "new eyes."
- A friendly response helps sustain children's interest in their writing.
- When conferring is part of a writing program, students learn how to talk about writing and how to receive and use information from others.

Major Concepts
- **Students with similar goals can help one another do their best writing.** (page 46)
- **Certain actions on the part of writers and responders promote successful conferences.** (page 47)
- **Students can confer throughout the writing process.** (page 48)
- **Writing down responses is a good way to help students gather their thoughts for a productive conference.** (page 49)

Performance Standards

Students are expected to . . .
- respond in constructive ways to others' writings.
- collaborate with other writers to generate ideas, compose, revise, and edit writing.

Getting Started with "Working with Partners"

Start-Up Activity: Ask students to suggest ways for partners to help each other from beginning to end in the writing process. Talk about ways a partner could help before the writing, during the writing, or when the writer is stuck. Then read "When to Work with Partners" on page 47 in the handbook. Compare this list to the ideas students generated.

Enrichment Activity: Give some students the opportunity to have a self-conference. Here are some questions a writer could ask himself or herself:

What have I said so far?
Which part shows my best work?
How does my writing sound?
What will my readers be thinking when they read this?

Teaching Resources

Write on Track Teacher's Guide

- Minilessons:
  "First You, Then Me" (page 210)
  "What I Like" (page 211)

Write on Track Handbook

- "Good-Listener Checklist," page 237, reminds students how to be careful listeners.

Write on Track Program Guide

- A teaching unit (lesson plans, blackline masters, and additional minilessons) can be found in the Program Guide ring binder.

Editing and Proofreading

(See handbook pages 50-51.)

"Editing and Proofreading" offers specific guidelines for preparing writing for publication. This final step in the writing process becomes important after the main ideas in the writing have been improved, or revised. The editing and proofreading checklist covers sentence clarity, word choice, punctuation, spelling, and capitalization.

Rationale
- Written work for public display needs to be correct.
- Errors make it difficult for readers to appreciate a piece of writing.
- Editing and proofreading one another's work helps develop a community of student writers.

Major Concepts
- **Editing and proofreading gets writing ready to be shared.** (page 50)
- **Editing and proofreading is a shared process.** (page 50)
- **A sentence check is an important part of editing.** (page 51)
- **Choosing interesting as well as correct words is an important editing skill.** (page 51)
- **Punctuation, spelling, and capitalization are important parts of proofreading.** (page 51)

Performance Standards

Students are expected to . . .
- edit drafts for features of polished writing such as appropriate grammar, spelling, capitalization, and punctuation.
- assess writing according to standards.

Getting Started with "Editing and Proofreading"

Start-Up Activity: Check "Publishing" in the Yellow Pages of a telephone book. There may be a publishing house in your area whose staff would be willing to talk to young "editors." Otherwise, consider inviting other people who use editing skills in their work: reporters, real estate agents, office managers, lawyers, engineers, architects, and so on.

Enrichment Activity: Ask students to guess how many different words mean "happy" and "sad." After they make an estimate, have them start listing synonyms on the chalkboard or an overhead. Then use a thesaurus to show the great variety of words available to writers and editors.

Teaching Resources

Write on Track Teacher's Guide

- Minilessons:

    "Editor in Chief" (page 211)

    "Two-Headed Editor" (page 211)

Write on Track Handbook

- "Proofreader's Guide," pages 292-337, has specific information about punctuation, capitalization, usage, and grammar.

Write on Track Program Guide

- A teaching unit (lesson plans, blackline masters, and additional minilessons) can be found in the Program Guide ring binder.

Publishing Your Writing

(See handbook pages 52-55.)

Publishing makes writing real, helps young writers get interested in their work, and creates a greater sense of pride and accomplishment. It underscores the importance of all the planning, drafting, and revising involved in the writing process. Publishing nurtures an awareness of authorship and audience, providing the writer with an opportunity to take center stage, to find out how well he or she is doing, and to learn how to do even better the next time.

Rationale
- Publishing is an integral part of the writing process.
- Seeing one's own work published builds self-esteem.
- Publishing promotes risk taking and paying closer attention to style, format, and language.

Major Concepts
- **Publishing is the last step in the writing process.** (page 52)
- **There are many ways to publish writing, including sharing a final draft with classmates.** (pages 53-55)

Performance Standards

> Students are expected to . . .
> - share finished pieces with classmates and others.

Getting Started with "Publishing Your Writing"

Start-Up Activity: Discuss the following statement with your students: "If you know your writing will be published, you will do your best work." Ask them why the prospect of publishing has a positive influence on a writer.

Enrichment Activity: Suggest that students search for Web sites where they can publish material related to their interests. Also have students prepare final copies of some of their favorite writings for publication in a classroom anthology.

Teaching Resources

Write on Track Teacher's Guide
- Minilessons:

  "Last Step, the Best Step" (page 211)

  "Group Authors" (page 212)

Write on Track Handbook
- "The Forms of Writing," pages 76-179, provides guidelines for various forms of writing that can be published.
- "Proofreader's Guide," pages 292-337, has specific information about punctuation, capitalization, usage, and grammar.

Write on Track Program Guide
- A teaching unit (lesson plans, blackline masters, and additional minilessons) can be found in the Program Guide ring binder.

Writing Paragraphs

(See handbook pages 57-65.)

A stand-alone paragraph presents a story, a description, an opinion, or an explanation about a specific subject. Writers choose one of these four paragraph types according to their subject and purpose for writing. No matter what form a paragraph takes, however, it needs enough supporting details to give readers a clear and interesting picture of the subject.

Rationale

- Authentic writing (news articles, directions to a specific place, requests) often involves the construction of simple paragraphs.
- Paragraphs are the conceptual building blocks for stories, essays, and articles. Writing paragraphs gives students the opportunity to think conceptually.
- When students understand the idea of "paragraph," they can better edit their work and find where their drafts need paragraph breaks.

Major Concepts

- **A paragraph is a group of sentences that tells about one specific subject or idea.** (page 57)
- **Paragraphs have three basic parts: topic sentence, body, closing sentence.** (pages 58-59)
- **The four types of paragraphs are based on their function: narrative, descriptive, expository, and persuasive.** (pages 60-63)
- **Writing a paragraph involves all the steps in the writing process.** (pages 64-65)

Performance Standards

Students are expected to . . .

- write a paragraph containing three or more sentences about the same subject.
- develop a topic sentence.
- include supporting facts.
- include a closing sentence that reminds readers of what the paragraph is about or leads to the next paragraph.

Getting Started with "Writing Paragraphs"

Start-Up Activity: When you hear a student telling a little story, jot it down as an example narrative. Do the same for a descriptive conversation shared on the playground, an expository moment when a student is explaining something, and a persuasive instance when a child is trying to convince someone of something. Relate these examples to the four types of paragraphs explained in this chapter.

Enrichment Activity: Have students write paragraphs about current, interesting subjects (social studies issues, science topics, class or schoolwide projects, recess activities, and so on).

Teaching Resources

Write on Track Teacher's Guide

- Minilessons:

  "Topic Sentences" (page 212)

  "Types of Paragraphs" (page 212)

- "Assessment Strategies and Rubrics" (pages 171-180)

Write on Track Handbook

- "The Forms of Writing," pages 76-179, provides guidelines for various forms of writing that can be published.

- "Proofreader's Guide," pages 292-337, has specific information about punctuation, capitalization, usage, and grammar.

Write on Track Program Guide

- A teaching unit (lesson plans, blackline masters, and additional minilessons) can be found in the Program Guide ring binder.

Writing a Summary

(See handbook pages 66-69.)

Summary writing helps students develop competence as critical thinkers and helps them integrate important reading and writing skills. As the handbook metaphor of "panning for gold" points out, when students write summaries, they are learning how to find the main ideas in reading material. Learning how to express these ideas succinctly in their own words is a valuable lifelong skill.

Rationale

- Summarizing helps students process information.
- Writing summaries helps students think more critically.
- Summary writing plays an important role in learning across the curriculum.

Major Concepts

- **Summarizing is a useful writing and learning skill.** (pages 66-67)
- **A summary writer must be a careful reader.** (page 68)
- **A summary should be written in the writer's own words.** (page 69)
- **The first sentence of a summary contains the most important idea.** (page 69)

Performance Standards

Students are expected to . . .
- write summaries that contain the most important information from a reading selection.

Getting Started with "Writing a Summary"

Start-Up Activity: With the class, do an oral summary of a well-known story (Cinderella, Beauty and the Beast, Jack and the Beanstalk). Try to keep the summary to five or six sentences, covering the most important parts of the story. Then have students, alone or in pairs, write their own summary of the story.

Enrichment Activity: Ask students to summarize special events: assemblies, class performances, field trips, classroom visitors, and so on. To build community ties, a monthly or quarterly "School Summary Sheet," using students' written summaries, could be sent home.

Teaching Resources

Write on Track Teacher's Guide
- Minilessons:
  " 'Amazing Hawks' " (page 213)
  "Smelly Business" (page 213)

Write on Track Handbook
- "Understanding the Parts of a Book," page 187, offers information that students could use when they are looking for the main ideas for a summary.

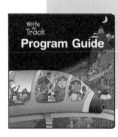

Write on Track Program Guide
- A teaching unit (lesson plans, blackline masters, and additional minilessons) can be found in the Program Guide ring binder.

Writing Basic Sentences

(See handbook pages 71-73.)

Sentences are building blocks of communication. We write sentences; we speak sentences; and we read them. Helping students develop their sentence sense must be a primary objective in any language arts curriculum. This objective can best be met by immersing students in the language. If they are engaged in all sorts of writing, reading, speaking, and listening activities, their sentence sense will develop naturally and effectively. To what extent you cover the technical aspects of sentences (naming the parts, identifying the different types, etc.) depends upon the needs of your students and the demands of your curriculum.

Rationale
- Students must develop their sentence sense in order to express themselves effectively.
- Students need a basic understanding of the grammar of sentences.

Major Concepts
- **Sentences are used all the time in writing, reading, and speaking.** (page 71)
- **A sentence is not complete unless it has a subject and a verb.** (page 72)
- **Fragments, run-ons, and rambling sentences are three common sentence problems.** (page 73)

Performance Standards

Students are expected to . . .
- apply standard English grammar and usage including subject-verb agreement.
- understand and be able to use complete and correct sentences of varying lengths.
- eliminate sentence fragments, run-on sentences, and rambling sentences with increasing accuracy.

Getting Started with "Writing Basic Sentences"

Start-Up Activity: List these subjects, predicates, and modifiers on the chalkboard:

Subjects	Predicates	Modifiers
The duck	swam	across the pond.
Uncle Max	flew	to Australia.
Samantha	limped	into the doctor's office.

Have the students find different ways to combine these sentence parts. Have fun!

Enrichment Activity: Create a game for partners called "Score Zero." Have pairs of students read some of their written work aloud. As one student reads, both students listen for fragments, run-on sentences, and rambling sentences. One point should be given for each sentence problem, but the purpose of the game is to score 0!

Teaching Resources

Write on Track Teacher's Guide

- Minilessons:

    "Sentence Tag" (page 213)

    "Neat and Complete" (page 214)

Write on Track Handbook

- "Combining Sentences," pages 74-75, takes students to the next level of writing sentences.

- "Making Your Story Come Alive," page 153, provides tips for using words and developing a writing voice.

- "Understanding Sentences," pages 322-325, defines basic sentence parts and shows how they work together.

Write on Track Program Guide

- A teaching unit (lesson plans, blackline masters, and additional minilessons) can be found in the Program Guide ring binder.

Combining Sentences

(See handbook pages 74-75.)

Most young writers need to focus on meaning and accuracy when they are writing sentences. Concern about the sound and flow of their sentences may be beyond them. But at some time during the school year, many students will be ready to learn about sentence combining. Combining gives young writers the chance to turn short, choppy statements into longer sentences that read more smoothly.

Rationale
- Stylistic writing is characterized by various combinations of long and short sentences.
- Sentence combining helps students see the variety of word combinations available to them.
- Sentence combining enhances students' editing skills.

Major Concepts
- **Sentence combining is making one longer sentence out of two or more short sentences.** (page 74)
- **Short sentences can be combined in many ways.** (page 75)

Performance Standards

Students are expected to . . .
- understand and be able to use complete and correct sentences of varying lengths.

Getting Started with "Combining Sentences"

Start-Up Activity: Write these three short sentences on the chalkboard:

> Apple pie is juicy.
> Apple pie is sweet.
> Apple pie is my favorite dessert.

Ask students to combine these three sentences into one sentence. Notice how many different ways they do this. Then have each student write three short sentences about a favorite food. Finally, have students combine their three short sentences into one.

Enrichment Activity: The next time students edit their writing, have them look for short, choppy sentences to combine.

Teaching Resources

Write on Track Teacher's Guide

- Minilessons:
  "And then . . . And then . . . " (page 214)
  "Let's eat!" (page 214)

Write on Track Handbook

- "Sentence Problems," page 73, helps students watch for sentence errors.
- "Types of Sentences," page 325, describes and models simple and compound sentences.

Write on Track Program Guide

- A teaching unit (lesson plans, blackline masters, and additional minilessons) can be found in the Program Guide ring binder.

The Forms of Writing

Introductory Notes

This section introduces "The Forms of Writing" chapters in the handbook and provides getting-started ideas to help you with your initial planning.

Writing in Journals

(See handbook pages 77-79.)

A journal can be a notebook with blank or lined pages. It can also be a stack of paper stapled together. Journals can hold students' observations, ideas about favorite topics and hobbies, and notes that can often be used in future writing tasks. Journal writing helps students discover their writing voices.

Rationale
- Students learn by writing.
- Fluency grows as students write regularly in journals. This fluency extends to other types of writing.
- Journal entries can serve as a resource for future writing tasks.

Major Concepts
- **Students can write in journals—just as their favorite authors do.** (page 77)
- **Students write about a variety of topics in personal journals.** (page 78)
- **In reading journals, students write about books they have read.** (page 79)

Performance Standards
Students are expected to . . .
- write to express, discover, record, develop, reflect on, and refine ideas.
- create journal entries as tools for learning.

Getting Started with "Writing in Journals"

Start-Up Activity: Share some of your own journal-writing experiences. Ask students about theirs—both positive and negative. Then share sections from a published journal, such as *Amelia's Notebook* by Marissa Moss. Read "Writing in a Personal Journal" on page 78 in the handbook. Allow class time for personal journaling on a regular basis, although not necessarily daily.

Enrichment Activity: Whenever your class has a celebration, goes on a field trip, has a special guest, and so on, have each student write a journal entry about it. Then bind the pages together and add photos or illustrations to create a special set of memoirs for your class library.

Teaching Resources

Write on Track Teacher's Guide

- Minilessons:

  "My Life!" (page 215)

  "Two R's: Readin' and Writin' " (page 215)

Write on Track Handbook

- "Tips for Writing to Learn," page 275, offers reminders for writing in a response journal.

Write on Track Program Guide

- A teaching unit (lesson plans, blackline masters, and additional minilessons) can be found in the Program Guide ring binder.

Making Albums

(See handbook pages 80-81.)

An album is a place for children to keep memories, a way to organize a special part of their lives. Collecting items in an album can give children a sense of control, satisfying a need to gather, arrange, and preserve.

Rationale
- Keeping an album gives students a fun way to practice organizational skills.
- Students are naturally inclined to collect items they care about.
- Students find a special appeal in arranging and writing about important memorabilia.

Major Concepts
- **There are many kinds of albums.** (page 80)
- **Following a three-step process, students can create thematic albums.** (page 81)

Performance Standards

Students are expected to . . .
- collect and record information about a topic.
- use anecdotes, descriptions, and vivid language to support ideas.

Getting Started with "Making Albums"

Start-Up Activity: Ask students to describe any scrapbooks or albums they have seen or made. Then read pages 80 and 81 in the handbook to prepare students for making individual or class albums. To practice writing captions, post two or three pictures in the front of the room and work with the class to write short, informative sentences about the pictures.

Enrichment Activity: Create a classroom album, dedicating one or two pages to each student. Allow students to use school photos, photos brought from home, drawings, and/or magazine pictures to make up their pages. In groups of two or three, have students write captions for their own pictures and for those of their group. Each student must then design his or her own pages and make the final caption decisions.

Teaching Resources

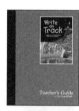

Write on Track Teacher's Guide
- Minilessons:
  "A Pet's Album" (page 215)
  "Tabby & Me" (page 215)

Write on Track Handbook
- "Writing Photo Essays," pages 142-147, offers additional ideas for putting pictures and text together.

Write on Track Program Guide
- A teaching unit (lesson plans, blackline masters, and additional minilessons) can be found in the Program Guide ring binder.

Writing Personal Narratives

(See handbook pages 82-85.)

Many experienced writers say that all writing begins with narrative. And the first stories, the most basic ones, come from an individual's own life. That is why it is so important, and so natural, to have your students write personal narratives throughout the school year. At first, your students will be most concerned with getting all of their facts and details straight. Then, as they become more experienced, they will also share feelings related to their personal stories. Watch for this development in the narratives they write.

Rationale
- Writing personal narratives helps children establish an identity and gain self-confidence.
- As they hear other children's personal narratives, they begin to identify with each other as well as understand each other's differences.

Major Concepts
- **A personal narrative is a story about a memorable event in the writer's life.** (pages 82-83)
- **Students can use the writing process to write personal narratives.** (pages 84-85)
- **Students can enrich their stories with details and dialogue.** (page 85)

Performance Standards - - - - -

Students are expected to . . .
- write narratives that recount personal experiences.
- use anecdotes, descriptions, and vivid language to support ideas.

Getting Started with "Writing Personal Narratives"

Start-Up Activity: All students (and teachers) have stories to tell. Have an informal sharing of "guess-what-happened" stories. To demonstrate what makes a story appealing, you may want to encourage stories about funny or unusual things that happened, and you may want to begin by telling a story of your own.

Enrichment Activity: Invite students to write one personal narrative for each year of their lives. Have them bind all the pages together into personal memory books.

Teaching Resources

Write on Track Teacher's Guide

- Minilessons:

  "Possum Tale" (page 215)

  "Strange Happenings" (page 216)

Write on Track Handbook

- "Traits of Good Writing," pages 18-21, is a useful reference for students as they develop their personal narratives.

Write on Track Program Guide

- A teaching unit (lesson plans, blackline masters, and additional minilessons) can be found in the Program Guide ring binder.

Writing Lists

(See handbook pages 86-89.)

Writing a list is a very accessible thinking activity. It can open a writer's mind and unlock ideas. Making a list can show the young writer, especially, that he or she has plenty to write about. Listing can also serve as a form of poetic expression.

Rationale
- Lists help students generate ideas.
- Lists help students organize their ideas.
- Lists promote logical and creative thinking.

Major Concepts
- **Lists can serve many useful purposes.** (page 86)
- **Lists can help writers remember, collect ideas, and think.** (pages 87-88)
- **Lists can help students tap into their creativity and have fun.** (pages 88-89)

Performance Standards
Students are expected to . . .
- create lists as tools for writing and learning.

Getting Started with "Writing Lists"

Start-Up Activity: Read the titles of the four kinds of listing activities on pages 86-89 in the handbook. Then focus on "Thinking in Different Ways" on page 88 and "Having Fun" on page 89. Begin a class "Happy List" and ask students to keep one of their own.

Enrichment Activity: Create your own classroom "Book of Lists." Create these lists as students begin studying new topics in social studies, science, music, math, art, and so on. When you have several lists, make copies and bind them together as reference books for students to use in the classroom.

Teaching Resources

Write on Track Teacher's Guide

- Minilessons:

  "Collecting Ideas" (page 216)

  "Happy Thoughts to You!" (page 216)

Write on Track Handbook

- "Choosing a Subject," pages 33-35, and "Gathering Details," pages 36-37, show how writing lists can be useful during the writing process.

- "Writing a List Poem," pages 171-172, provides guidelines for writing a list poem.

Write on Track Program Guide

- A teaching unit (lesson plans, blackline masters, and additional minilessons) can be found in the Program Guide ring binder.

Writing Friendly Notes

(See handbook pages 90-93.)

Friendly notes are quick and easy to write. Whether they're sent by traditional mail or by e-mail, there is a directness to writing notes to friends and acquaintances. Notes and e-mail messages are more user-friendly than traditional friendly letters.

Rationale
- Writing friendly notes and e-mail messages gives children the opportunity to write spontaneously about topics they care about.
- Friendly notes and e-mail messages usually elicit immediate feedback from the recipients.
- Writing can be a way to cement friendships.

Major Concepts
- **Friendly notes and e-mail messages are fun for the writer and the recipient.** (page 90)
- **Friendly notes are short and varied in format.** (page 90)
- **People write friendly notes and e-mail messages for a variety of reasons.** (pages 91-93)

Performance Standards
Students are expected to . . .
- correspond with peers or others via e-mail, conventional mail, or friendly notes.

Getting Started with "Writing Friendly Notes"

Start-Up Activity: Read about the differences between a friendly note (or e-mail) and a friendly letter on page 90 in the handbook. Then talk about four reasons for writing friendly notes—to say thank you, to ask a favor, to send a special message, and to give a reminder. Have each student write a friendly note to a staff member of your school. Give students time to write and decorate their messages.

Enrichment Activity: Have rotating note-writing committees in your classroom. Ask the members of the committee to write thank-you notes and reminders whenever they are needed. Encourage the members of the committee to not only look for occasions for writing but also for special paper and note formats.

Teaching Resources

Write on Track Teacher's Guide

- Minilessons:

  "Apples for the Teacher" (page 216)

  "Notes to You!" (page 217)

Write on Track Handbook

- "Writing Friendly Letters," pages 94-97, "Letter to the Editor," page 113, and "Writing Business Letters," pages 126-133, give students practice in other forms of letter writing.

Write on Track Program Guide

- A teaching unit (lesson plans, blackline masters, and additional minilessons) can be found in the Program Guide ring binder.

Writing Friendly Letters

(See handbook pages 94-97.)

The friendly letter is a natural form of writing for students. Like all of us, children enjoy getting personal mail, and they learn quickly that the best way to get a letter is to send one.

Rationale
- Writing a friendly letter gives children the opportunity to write about topics they care about.
- Receiving letters encourages students to write more.
- Learning how to communicate in writing is an important social skill.
- Letter writing promotes fluency in all writing.

Major Concepts
- **A friendly letter has a heading, salutation, body, closing, and signature.** (pages 94-95)
- **Good letters result from planning and revising.** (pages 96-97)

Performance Standards

Students are expected to . . .
- correspond with peers or others via e-mail, conventional mail, or friendly notes.
- write friendly letters that consider audience, purpose, and context.
- write friendly letters that include all the parts of a letter.
- write friendly letters that have a correctly addressed envelope.

Getting Started with "Writing Friendly Letters"

Start-Up Activity: Poll the class to find out how many students have received a personal letter or postcard through the mail. Also find out how many have sent letters. Then, with students' input, create a list of reasons to write letters. Some reasons might include sharing news, wishing someone a happy birthday, asking a favorite author a question, and so on.

Enrichment Activity: It's important and fun to have a variety of people to write friendly letters to. To suggest possible correspondents and encourage ongoing writing, have students list friends, relatives, and authors they might want to write to during the school year.

Teaching Resources

Write on Track Teacher's Guide

- Minilessons:

  "Custodians and Secretaries" (page 217)

  "Five-Part Harmony" (page 217)

Write on Track Handbook

- "Letter to the Editor," page 113, and "Writing Business Letters," pages 126-133, give students practice in other forms of letter writing.

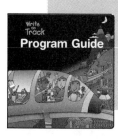

Write on Track Program Guide

- A teaching unit (lesson plans, blackline masters, and additional minilessons) can be found in the Program Guide ring binder.

Writing Family Stories

(See handbook pages 98-101.)

Family stories show us how families are unique, and, on the other hand, how much they have in common. Families tell stories over and over again to inspire, to inform, and to entertain. These are the stories that help identify a family. Students should be aware that in crafting family stories, they are preserving something priceless.

Rationale
- Writing "familiar" stories offers a natural starting point for working with story structure.
- Retelling a story helps young writers learn to organize information and sequence events.

Major Concepts
- **Family stories can express every emotion.** (page 98)
- **A family story can come from a writer's own experience or from a story told by a relative.** (page 99)
- **Students can learn to write a family story using the writing process.** (pages 100-101)

Performance Standards

Students are expected to . . .
- write narratives that recount personal experiences.
- use anecdotes, descriptions, and vivid language to support ideas.

Getting Started with "Writing Family Stories"

Start-Up Activity: Many authors favored by young readers write family stories. Picture books like *A Birthday Basket for Tia* by Pat Mora, *The Moon Lady* by Amy Tan, *My Great-Aunt Arizona* by Gloria Houston, *The Wednesday Surprise* by Eve Bunting, and *Tea with Milk* by Allen Say (or any other favorite family stories) give students a good sampling of the different kinds of family tales in print.

Enrichment Activity: In this era of mobility, many children hear about faraway places where their grandparents and parents were born or have traveled. These birthplace and travel stories offer opportunities for students to do some research and map study.

Teaching Resources

Write on Track Teacher's Guide

- Minilessons:
    "Animal Families" (page 217)
    "All in the Family" (page 217)

Write on Track Handbook

- "Learning to Interview," pages 252-255, gives students tips for gathering information directly from their subjects.

Write on Track Program Guide

- A teaching unit (lesson plans, blackline masters, and additional minilessons) can be found in the Program Guide ring binder.

Writing Alphabet Books

(See handbook pages 103-107.)

Poet Norma Farber calls alphabet books her love letters to children. Teachers who introduce such love letters into their curriculum quickly discover a marvelous tool for encouraging independent and creative thinking. The alphabet offers a framework to which young writers and illustrators can add thoughtful words and a variety of illustrations.

Rationale
- The ABC format encourages students to have fun with language.
- The ABC format gives students a way to organize information.

Major Concepts
- **Nearly any subject can be understood by arranging its main ideas or components in ABC order.** (page 103)
- **Writing alphabet books is fun and challenging.** (page 104)
- **Students use the writing process to compose an alphabet book.** (pages 105-107)

Performance Standards

Students are expected to . . .
- collect information about a subject.
- record their own knowledge of a subject in a variety of ways—by drawing pictures, making lists, and showing connections between ideas.

Getting Started with "Writing Alphabet Books"

Start-Up Activity: Provide alphabet books for students to examine and enjoy. Be sure to include some with sophisticated content and illustrations, assuring students that alphabet books are not just for little children. Read and enjoy the alphabet book samples on pages 104 and 107 in the handbook. Then assist students in choosing subjects and doing research for the alphabet books they will create. Have them follow the steps of the writing process on pages 105-106.

Enrichment Activity: Create a class ABC book with each student responsible for one or two letters of the alphabet. The book could focus on a holiday theme or study topic in social studies, science, math, art, or health. Decide together on the format and type of illustrations you will use. You may want to develop a template for this group book.

Teaching Resources

Write on Track Teacher's Guide

- Minilessons:

 "Knowing Your A's and B's" (page 218)

 "Getting a Little Crazy!" (page 218)

Write on Track Handbook

- "Making Pleasing Sounds," page 173, encourages students to be aware of the sounds of their words.

Write on Track Program Guide

- A teaching unit (lesson plans, blackline masters, and additional minilessons) can be found in the Program Guide ring binder.

Writing Newspaper Stories

(See handbook pages 108-113.)

Third-grade students are often very eager to reach out to an audience with their writing. A classroom newspaper provides the perfect format to inspire these young writers.

Rationale
- The real-world nature of newspaper writing gives it importance.
- Newspaper writing emphasizes the qualities of good writing—clarity, coherence, and accuracy.

Major Concepts
- **A news story has a specific structure.** (pages 109, 111)
- **A newswriter has the responsibility to collect information.** (page 110)
- **News and human-interest stories need strong leads.** (pages 109, 111-112)
- **Writing a letter to the editor is an important way to practice freedom of expression and freedom of the press.** (page 113)

Performance Standards

Students are expected to . . .
- write news stories that contain a lead, or beginning, giving the most important idea.
- write news stories that contain a body, or middle, telling more about the story.
- write new stories that contain an ending, giving the reader an idea to remember.

Getting Started with "Writing Newspaper Stories"

Start-Up Activity: To familiarize students with newswriting vocabulary, distribute news stories from grade-level news magazines to pairs or small groups of students. Have the groups compare the parts of their stories to the sample news story on page 109 in the handbook.

Enrichment Activity: After they have written a few news stories, human-interest stories, and/or letters to editors, encourage students to develop their own classroom newspaper.

Teaching Resources

Write on Track Teacher's Guide

- Minilessons:

    "Getting Down to Basics" (page 218)

    "In My Opinion" (page 219)

Write on Track Handbook

- "Descriptive Paragraph," page 61, gives students ideas for collecting information about a person, a place, or an object.
- "Persuasive Paragraph," page 63, presents a model of writing that would transfer well to writing editorials.
- "Using Facts and Opinions Correctly" and "Sticking to the Facts," pages 271-273, remind students about how facts and opinions differ.

Write on Track Program Guide

- A teaching unit (lesson plans, blackline masters, and additional minilessons) can be found in the Program Guide ring binder.

Writing Book Reviews

(See handbook pages 114-119.)

A book review answers questions that readers often wonder about before they decide to read a book. Most students like to know what books their friends are reading and what the books are about. Students will enjoy writing and reading book reviews if the right tone is set in the classroom.

Rationale
- Book reviews give students opportunities to write about books they care about.
- Book reviews give students opportunities to write persuasively.
- Writing book reviews brings reading and writing skills together and demonstrates comprehension.

Major Concepts
- **A book review provides an opportunity to share feelings.** (page 114)
- **A basic book review answers these three questions: (1) What is the book about? (2) Why do I like this book? (3) What main idea does the author share?** (pages 115-118)
- **Reviewers use a special vocabulary when they talk about books.** (page 119)

Performance Standards

Students are expected to . . .
- demonstrate an understanding of a literary work.
- support judgments about a book through references to the text or to personal knowledge.

Getting Started with "Writing Book Reviews"

Start-Up Activity: Give students a few days' notice to bring a favorite picture book or novel to school. When everyone has a book, place students in groups of five or six. Have each student take a turn answering the following questions: What is the book about? Why do I like the book? What main idea or message does the author share in the book?

Enrichment Activity: Have each student choose a character from a fiction book. Designate a day when students should bring an artifact related to the character, an article of clothing, a hat, or a mask to portray the character. Then have each student introduce himself or herself in the persona of the character. Encourage questions from the class to the character about his or her life.

Teaching Resources

Write on Track Teacher's Guide
- Minilessons:

    "The Big Three" (page 219)

    "Words About Books" (page 219)

Write on Track Handbook
- "Writing Plays," pages 160-165, may help students understand some of the "Elements of Literature," page 119.

Write on Track Program Guide
- A teaching unit (lesson plans, blackline masters, and additional minilessons) can be found in the Program Guide ring binder.

Test Your FLEXIBILITY

1 First, stand up and put your feet together.

2 Next, bend slowly at the waist and try to touch the floor in front of your toes. Don't bend your knees . . . or bounce!

How-To Writing

(See handbook pages 120-125.)

Young students can probably tell someone how to do something, but writing an explanation may be new for them. It is important that they begin practicing how-to writing, since this form will be required of them as they advance in school. In social studies, they may be asked to explain how early settlers in their area provided for themselves; in science, how the water cycle works; and in math, how they solved a certain problem.

Rationale
- How-to writing helps students organize their thoughts.
- How-to writing helps students sequence ideas and write clearly and precisely.
- How-to writing, such as giving directions, has practical applications for students.

Major Concepts
- **How-to writing (an explanation) begins with a topic sentence (or descriptive title), followed by clear, step-by-step directions.** (pages 120-125)
- **Action words (*put, stand, take*) in how-to writing tell the reader what to do.** (page 121)
- **Order words (*next, then, after*) help the reader follow each step.** (page 121)

Performance Standards
Students are expected to . . .
- write directions that identify the sequence of steps needed to do something or to get somewhere.

Getting Started with "How-To Writing"

Start-Up Activity: Compile a list of relatively simple things that students know how to do well (ride a two-wheeler, make popcorn, play baseball, and so on). Place students in small groups of two or three, according to the thing they do well. (There can be more than one group per activity.) Have students tell one another the exact directions for doing their activities. Then read about the process for writing directions on pages 121-122 in the handbook. Each group should appoint a "secretary" to write down the directions in the proper order. Finally, share the directions with the class to see if they make sense.

Enrichment Activity: Turn to "How-To Writing" in the handbook. Invite students to choose a "how-to" topic like cooking, a summer or winter sport, a science experiment, caring for pets, creating a Web page, and so on. Individuals or small groups should then compile a manual for the chosen topic. Encourage the writers to include illustrations and diagrams.

Teaching Resources

Write on Track Teacher's Guide
- Minilessons:
  "Robotics" (page 219)
  "Left at the Stoplight" (page 220)

Write on Track Handbook
- "Expository Paragraph," page 62, explains the basics of expository writing.
- Study any of the writing guidelines throughout the handbook as models of explaining how to write different forms of writing.

Write on Track Program Guide
- A teaching unit (lesson plans, blackline masters, and additional minilessons) can be found in the Program Guide ring binder.

Writing Business Letters

(See handbook pages 126-133.)

The business letter may be a new writing form for many of your students. It adds a real-life element to the classroom as students write letters to request information or suggest solutions to problems, and then experience the excitement of getting mail in return.

Rationale
- The business letter is a real-world writing form that students can use to get information or to suggest certain actions.
- As students receive serious responses to well-planned and carefully written letters, they will appreciate the power of the written word.
- The ability to write a clear business letter is a valuable lifelong skill.

Major Concepts
- **Two types of business letters are introduced—a letter asking for information and a letter suggesting how to solve a problem.** (pages 127, 129, 132)
- **Business letters have a common format: heading, inside address, salutation, body, closing, and signature.** (pages 128-129)
- **Writing a business letter is a step-by-step process.** (pages 130-131)
- **There is an accepted way to fold and address a business letter.** (page 133)

Performance Standards

Students are expected to write a business letter that . . .
- includes all parts of a letter.
- considers audience and purpose.
- has a correctly addressed envelope.

Getting Started with "Writing Business Letters"

Start-Up Activity: Write a business letter, as a class, to someone who will hopefully reply promptly. Plan and write the first draft on the chalkboard, using the sample letter and guidelines on pages 129-131 in the handbook. Use students' suggestions for the content of the letter. Ask a volunteer to prepare a final copy of the letter to send.

Enrichment Activity: Invite students to set up a business-letter bulletin board showing a large version of a business letter (and envelope if you wish) with all the parts labeled. Include a place for posting responses, and a chart showing the state and provincial abbreviations.

Teaching Resources

Write on Track Teacher's Guide

- Minilessons:

  "Why Write?" (page 220)

  "And the Envelope, Please" (page 220)

Write on Track Handbook

- "Using E-Mail," page 189, offers a model e-mail message, a type of writing used frequently in today's business world.

Write on Track Program Guide

- A teaching unit (lesson plans, blackline masters, and additional minilessons) can be found in the Program Guide ring binder.

Writing Classroom Reports

(See handbook pages 135-141.)

Writing classroom reports can be a fascinating introduction to independent thinking, searching, and exploring. Students' own curiosity becomes their most valuable research tool. After finding subjects that truly interest them, young writer-researchers can follow certain steps that will lead to successful classroom reports.

Rationale

- Report writing taps into students' natural curiosity.
- Report writing helps students understand how nonfiction material can be organized.
- Knowing methods for keeping track of information is a valuable lifelong skill.

Major Concepts

- **It's important for writers to choose topics they care about.** (pages 135-137)
- **Asking good questions is a key to successful report writing.** (pages 136-139)
- **A gathering grid organizes information.** (page 138)
- **Writers should begin their reports in a way that hooks the reader.** (page 139)

Performance Standards

Students are expected to . . .
- write classroom reports with a beginning that introduces the subject.
- write classroom reports with a middle that answers questions about the subject.
- write classroom reports with an ending that includes an important idea about the subject.

Getting Started with "Writing Classroom Reports"

Start-Up Activity: Read the introduction to the chapter and the report "Amazing Hawks" on pages 135 and 144 in the handbook. With students' input, make a list of interesting subjects they could use for report writing. (Be sure to include science or social studies topics from your curriculum.) Then discuss the term *research.* Explain to students that their research can involve textbooks, classroom or school library books, magazines, the Internet, and interviews with knowledgeable persons.

Enrichment Activity: List several research questions that will send students to a variety of sources to find the answers. The questions should lead students to reference books in the classroom or library, the Internet, or other accessible authorities. (Students may enjoy working in teams for this activity.)

Teaching Resources

Write on Track Teacher's Guide
- Minilessons:

  "Getting Started" (page 220)

  "Getting a Grip on a Grid" (page 221)

Write on Track Handbook
- "Using the Library," pages 181-187, has many practical guidelines for students who will be doing research in the library.
- "Using the Internet," pages 188-193, gives tips about using the Internet for research.
- "Making a Multimedia Slide Show," pages 250-251, shows students how an oral presentation (short talk) is turned into a multimedia presentation.

Write on Track Program Guide
- A teaching unit (lesson plans, blackline masters, and additional minilessons) can be found in the Program Guide ring binder.

Writing Photo Essays

(See handbook pages 142-147.)

Author Myra Zarnowski says photo essays are the "show-and-tell" of writing. Using photos and words, writers can show and tell readers about people, places, animals, and more.

Rationale
- Most children enjoy photo essays.
- Learning how photos and text work together taps children's thinking skills.
- Photo essays require research and decision making.
- The photo essay requires maintaining a focus, which is a valuable organizational skill.

Major Concepts
- **Photo essays are the show-and-tell of writing.** (pages 142, 144)
- **Photo essays need to have a beginning, a middle, and an ending.** (pages 143-145)
- **A photo essay requires research.** (page 146)
- **The pictures and words in a photo essay need to match.** (page 147)

Performance Standards

Students are expected to . . .
- collect information about a subject.
- write to express, record, and reflect on ideas.

Getting Started with "Writing Photo Essays"

Start-Up Activity: Share a photo essay with your students. (See page 190 in this guide for a list of photo essays or choose one from a magazine like *Ranger Rick*.) Point out how words alone give only part of the "picture." Then read together the chapter introduction and the sample essay on pages 143-145. Discuss other pictures and captions the authors of this essay might have included. Tell students they will be doing photo essays about a school project (possibly one essay for the whole class, or several essays done in small groups).

Enrichment Activity: Throughout the year, photograph class holiday programs, science fairs, or field trips. Give these photos to small groups to create photo essays about their classroom experiences. If possible, place the essays in the school library for students' enjoyment over the next few years.

Teaching Resources

Write on Track Teacher's Guide

- Minilessons:
  "Before, During, After" (page 221)
  "Photo Shoot" (page 221)

Write on Track Handbook

- "Making Albums," pages 80-81, provides ideas for working with pictures and text.

Write on Track Program Guide

- A teaching unit (lesson plans, blackline masters, and additional minilessons) can be found in the Program Guide ring binder.

Writing Realistic Stories

(See handbook pages 149-153.)

Realistic stories are based on real life—things that do or could happen. This genre of children's literature has grown exponentially over the past several decades, so today's young readers have a wide variety of books to choose from. A strong interest in social issues affecting our multicultural citizenry, other adults, people with disabilities, and others has also contributed to the revolution in this genre.

Rationale	• Children find a ready source of realistic-story ideas in their own life experience.
	• Writing from a make-believe character's point of view, or about a slightly altered problem, gives children the distance to reflect upon their own lives and times.

Major Concepts	• **Realistic stories are about believable people and events.** (page 149)
	• **A realistic story must have a problem that needs to be solved.** (pages 150-151)
	• **First drafts can begin with real characters, problems, settings, and then be changed into made-up stories.** (page 152)

Performance Standards - - - - -

> Students are expected to . . .
> • write made-up narratives that are based on real experiences.
> • use vivid language to express ideas.
> • share finished work with classmates and others.

Getting Started with "Writing Realistic Stories"

Start-Up Activity: Read "A Very Far Hit" on page 150 in the handbook. Explain that this story of realistic fiction is based on a true story with some made-up sections added. (Have students consider which parts might be fiction.)

List some interesting and fun events that have happened recently at school. Choose one of these events to write a class story about. Next, read "Make Things Up" on page 152 in the handbook. With these ideas in mind, have students (as individuals or in a group), make realistic changes to the class story. Share the students' different versions based on the same event.

Enrichment Activity: Using their completed realistic stories, have students create scripts for a puppet show, a reader's theater performance, or another kind of dramatic presentation. (See pages 163-165 in the handbook for help with writing a script.)

Teaching Resources

Write on Track Teacher's Guide

- Minilessons:

  "At the End" (page 221)

  "You Don't Say" (page 222)

Write on Track Handbook

- "Writing Personal Narratives," pages 82-85, may give students ideas for their stories.
- "Telling Stories," pages 256-261, may help students find a story to write.

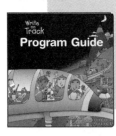

Write on Track Program Guide

- A teaching unit (lesson plans, blackline masters, and additional minilessons) can be found in the Program Guide ring binder.

Writing Time-Travel Fantasies

(See handbook pages 154-159.)

Children often invent imaginative scenarios as they play. One day they are defending a castle, and the next they are preparing to blast off into space. When children channel these creative energies into story writing, they can produce wonderful finished products.

Rationale

- When writing time-travel fantasies, students have a chance to learn about other times and places.
- Fantasy writing fosters three important creative thinking skills—flexibility, originality, and elaboration.

Major Concepts

- **Writing a fantasy often begins with asking "what if" questions.** (page 154)
- **When a story takes place in another time, it's important to learn about that time in order to create a believable setting.** (page 155)
- **The characters in a time-travel fantasy need a way to get to their new destination.** (page 155)
- **In addition to a setting, a time-travel fantasy needs characters who have a problem to solve.** (page 156)

Performance Standards

Students are expected to . . .
- write narratives that are based on fantasy.
- use vivid language and details to support ideas.
- share finished work with classmates and others.

Getting Started with "Time-Travel Fantasies"

Start-Up Activity: Read the introduction on page 154, along with the sample story on pages 158-159 in the handbook. Connect this information to time-travel books and videos familiar to the students. Then read about prewriting on page 156. Brainstorm for interesting places, characters, and problems for the students' fantasies.

Enrichment Activity: In contrast to the handbook, where the students are asked to write about a character traveling into the past or the future, give students the opportunity to write about a character from the past, coming to visit the present. Begin the discussion by introducing a well-known historical figure to the class. Talk about what this person's present-day visit would be like. Encourage students to write this kind of time-travel story.

Teaching Resources

Write on Track Teacher's Guide

- Minilessons:

  "Way Back When" (page 222)

  "A Problem in Time" (page 222)

Write on Track Handbook

- "Make Your Story Come Alive," page 152, reminds students of ways to enliven their fantasies.

- "Publishing Your Writing," pages 52-55, provides suggestions for students who wish to share their fantasies outside the classroom.

- "Telling Stories," pages 256-261, may help students find a story to write.

Write on Track Program Guide

- A teaching unit (lesson plans, blackline masters, and additional minilessons) can be found in the Program Guide ring binder.

Writing Plays

(See handbook pages 160-165.)

Writing a play can be an inviting experience for children, especially if the play is based on a familiar fairy tale or fable. Young children often create impromptu plays in school and in their free time. Learning how to write a script will offer them a chance to preserve their plays.

Rationale
- Writing scripts is an outlet for students' natural speaking skills.
- Plays are made up of dialogue—a form of language that third graders know as "the way people talk."
- Writing plays, which are meant to be performed, provides students with a keen awareness of an audience for their writing.

Major Concepts
- **Plays, like stories, have settings, characters, and problems to be solved.** (page 160)
- **Plays use a special format.** (page 161)
- **A play is a story that unfolds in scenes acted out by characters (actors) who memorize the written script.** (pages 162-165)

Performance Standards

Students are expected to . . .
- invent characters, a problem, and a setting for a play.
- create dialogue for characters.
- share finished work with classmates and others.

Getting Started with "Writing Plays"

Start-Up Activity: Do an improvisation of the fairy tale "The Three Little Pigs." Introduce the terms *scene, setting, dialogue,* and *characters.* Use these terms as you choose volunteers for the improvisation. Then have fun!

When you begin working with the chapter, compare the scene from "The Three Little Pigs" on page 161 in the handbook with your class improvisation.

Enrichment Activity: Have students write their own surprise endings to their favorite fairy-tale plays. In "Cinderella," Prince Charming might marry one of the stepsisters, or in "The Three Bears," Goldilocks could become Baby Bear's baby-sitter.

Teaching Resources

Write on Track Teacher's Guide

- Minilessons:

  "Play Along" (page 222)

  "Talk! Talk! Talk!" (page 222)

Write on Track Handbook

- "Make Your Story Come Alive," page 152, reminds students of ways to keep their plays moving.

Write on Track Program Guide

- A teaching unit (lesson plans, blackline masters, and additional minilessons) can be found in the Program Guide ring binder.

Writing Free-Verse Poetry

(See handbook pages 167-173.)

Seeing, hearing, and feeling the language of poetry is what free-verse poetry is all about. Several poets tell us why. Remembering the first poem she ever heard, Georgia Heard states, "It was about silver scales of fish and the ripples of water in a pond. I was astonished at what it made me see." When thinking about poetry, Myra Cohn Livingston talks of seeing oneself in a poem—feeling the language of poetry.

Rationale
- As students write poetry, they explore personal and creative avenues for expressing their ideas, feelings, and imaginings.
- Writing poetry gives students practice in capturing sights, sounds, and feelings in words.

Major Concepts
- **Everyone can write poems.** (page 167)
- **Writers of poetry are usually also readers of poetry.** (page 168)
- **Poetry looks and sounds different from prose.** (page 169)
- **Free-verse poetry can be long or short and does not have to rhyme.** (page 170)
- **Students can use the writing process to write poetry.** (pages 171-172)
- **Repeating sounds, similes, and metaphors add a special touch to poetry.** (page 173)

Performance Standards

Students are expected to . . .
- write poems that reflect an awareness of the pleasing sounds of language.
- write poems that express feelings and/or capture sights and sounds in a few words.

Getting Started with "Writing Free-Verse Poetry"

Start-Up Activity: Share a collection of poems and poetry books. Find and read free-verse poems rather than traditional forms. Invite students to read or recite poems they know and like. Note how their choices compare to free-verse poetry. Then read and share the ideas about free-verse poetry on pages 167-170 in the handbook.

Enrichment Activity: As each season begins, invite students to write poems related to that time of year. Have them illustrate their poems and display them on a bulletin board or other dedicated space.

Teaching Resources

Write on Track Teacher's Guide

- Minilessons:

   " 'When I Grow Up' " (page 223)

   "Making Comparisons" (page 223)

Write on Track Handbook

- "Publishing Your Writing," pages 52-55, gives students ideas and outlets for sharing their poetry.
- "Performing Poems," pages 238-243, is a natural follow-up to "Writing Free-Verse Poetry."

Write on Track Program Guide

- A teaching unit (lesson plans, blackline masters, and additional minilessons) can be found in the Program Guide ring binder.

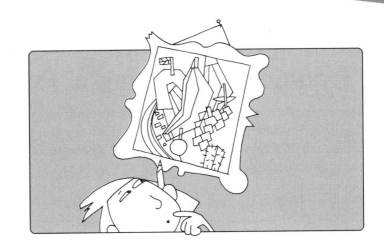

Traditional and Playful Poetry

(See handbook pages 174-179.)

Both traditional and playful poetic forms offer structures that students can mimic. Whether they are attempting a traditional cinquain or haiku, a playful alphabet or concrete poem, children will find a framework for their imaginative ideas.

Rationale
- Young children enjoy traditional poetry with its rhyme, rhythm, and predictable structure.
- Working with haiku encourages keen observation and careful word choice.
- Writing limericks offers the release of humor while challenging students to follow a regular pattern of rhyme and rhythm.
- Playful forms can encourage the reluctant student to give poetry writing a try.

Major Concepts
- **Traditional forms of poetry include, among others, cinquain, haiku, and limerick.** (page 175)
- **Haiku links nature to the writer's thoughts.** (pages 175-177)
- **"Playful poetry" demonstrates that language can be fun.** (pages 178-179)

Performance Standards
Students are expected to . . .
- write poems that reflect an awareness of pleasing sounds.
- write poems that express feelings and/or capture sights and sounds in words.

Getting Started with "Traditional and Playful Poetry"

Start-Up Activity: Have volunteers (including yourself) read or recite a favorite poem for the class. Following the poetry presentations, read about traditional and playful poetry on pages 174-175 and 178 in the handbook. Choose one of the forms on these pages and write a poem as a class.

Enrichment Activity: Have students write poetry using the forms and information on pages 175-179 in the handbook. When students (or pairs of students) have a small collection of original poems, they can create poetry books. (A personally illustrated, bound book will make a nice keepsake.)

Teaching Resources

Write on Track Teacher's Guide

- Minilessons:

  "Detective Poems" (page 223)

  "All Decked Out" (page 223)

Write on Track Handbook

- "Publishing Your Writing," pages 52-55, gives students ideas and outlets for sharing their poetry.
- "Performing Poems," pages 238-243, is a natural follow-up to "Traditional and Playful Poetry."

Write on Track Program Guide

- A teaching unit (lesson plans, blackline masters, and additional minilessons) can be found in the Program Guide ring binder.

The Tools of Learning

Introductory Notes

This section introduces "The Tools of Learning" chapters in the handbook and provides getting-started ideas to help you with your initial planning.

Using the Library

(See handbook pages 181-187.)

The library may seem overwhelming to some students, but once they learn basic library skills, they'll be ready to take advantage of everything the library has to offer. When it comes to students and libraries, familiarity breeds learning and fun.

Rationale
- Libraries are information storehouses that students need to learn how to use.
- Once students understand how the library works, they can become skillful researchers.

Major Concepts
- **Libraries contain books and many other media.** (page 181)
- **Knowing how to use the card catalog and/or computer catalog helps students identify sources of information.** (pages 182-184)
- **Understanding how books are shelved helps students find the specific books they need.** (page 185)
- **Encyclopedias and other reference books contain information on a wide variety of subjects.** (page 186)
- **Understanding the parts of books helps students use these resources more effectively.** (page 187)

Performance Standards

Students are expected to . . .
- use print and electronic sources to locate books.
- understand and be able to use the table of contents, chapter and section headings, the glossary, and the index to locate information in a reference book.
- understand the appropriate use of reference materials.

Getting Started with "Using the Library"

Start-Up Activity: Write the following heading on the board: What I Know About the Library. Have students volunteer ideas. Then have them brainstorm for ideas related to this heading: What I Want to Learn About the Library. This information should help you assess students' knowledge of the library.

Enrichment Activity: Have students present oral reports using details found in the "other reference books" listed on page 186 of the handbook.

Teaching Resources

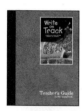

Write on Track Teacher's Guide

- Minilessons:

    "One Way or Another" (page 224)

    "Parts of a Book" (page 224)

Write on Track Handbook

- "Using the Internet," pages 188-193, introduces and explains this important source of information.

Write on Track Program Guide

- A teaching unit (lesson plans, blackline masters, and additional minilessons) can be found in the Program Guide ring binder.

Using the Internet

(See handbook pages 188-193.)

The Internet connects you and your students to people and information all around the world. It is an electronic post office and the biggest library in the world. The Internet offers countless opportunities for researching as well as writing and publishing ideas. Students, however, need to acquire certain skills to make these connections on the World Wide Web.

Rationale
- Internet skills are useful, if not imperative, for today's students.
- E-mail exchanges enhance the excitement of sharing written greetings and information with others in a potentially worldwide audience.
- Real-world activities, such as exploring Web sites for information and submitting writing for publication, get students interested and keep them involved.

Major Concepts
- **The Internet connects computers around the world.** (page 188)
- **E-mail messages are a quick and easy way to write to others.** (page 189)
- **The World Wide Web enables access to the information sources of the Internet including on-line encyclopedias, electronic libraries, and search engines.** (pages 190-192)
- **Web manners called "Netiquette" give guidelines for good behavior.** (page 193)

Performance Standards

Students are expected to . . .
- use available technology to support aspects of creating, revising, editing, and publishing texts.

Getting Started with "Using the Internet"

Start-Up Activity: Find out if any students in your class have designed their own Web sites or helped to design Web sites. Invite the Webmasters to share their experiences. Prepare printouts of Web pages from sites that reflect your students' interests or deal with topics you have been studying in class. Discuss several sites. If students would like to know more about creating a Web page, direct them to <thewritesource.com> and the "Web Design" link.

Enrichment Activity: Give students opportunities to get homework help and to do research on-line. Direct them to "Research Links" and "Other Links" listed at <thewritesource.com> to get them started.

Teaching Resources

Write on Track Teacher's Guide

- Minilesson:

    "Emoticons" (page 224)

Write on Track Handbook

- "Writing with a Computer," pages 22-27, gives students tips for using computers.

Write on Track Program Guide

- A teaching unit (lesson plans, blackline masters, and additional minilessons) can be found in the Program Guide ring binder.

Reading Graphics

(See handbook pages 195-199.)

Graphics are among the oldest forms of written communication. In fact, the first written languages used graphics, not letters or words. To read graphics means to understand symbols, diagrams, tables, and other kinds of pictorial information.

Rationale
- Students need to know how to understand common graphics found in classroom materials, in public information, and in different media.
- The skills needed to "read" graphics and other visual forms of information differ from those needed to read text.

Major Concepts
- **Graphics give information and help students learn.** (page 195)
- **Symbols are simple graphics that stand for something.** (page 196)
- **Diagrams are graphics that show the parts of something, or how something works.** (page 197)
- **Bar graphs are graphics used to compare two or more things.** (page 198)
- **Tables are graphics that organize numbers and words to give information quickly, as in a schedule.** (page 199)

Performance Standards
Students are expected to . . .
- read, understand, and present information in various forms.

Getting Started with "Reading Graphics"

Start-Up Activity: Have students trace one of their hands. Then ask them to think of labels—"thumb," "forefinger," "fingernails," and so on—for their drawings. When the pictures are completed, ask volunteers to share their drawings with the class. Explain that these diagrams are a kind of graphic.

Enrichment Activity: Students can create bar graphs or tables related to procedures that take place in the classroom. Consider a graphic to show how extracurricular activities and the regular classroom schedule work together. (This may be a beneficial activity for students who periodically leave the regular classroom for special classes.)

Teaching Resources

Write on Track Teacher's Guide
- Minilessons:
  "Picture Talk" (page 224)
  "On the Table" (page 225)

Write on Track Handbook
- "Student Almanac," pages 338-391, includes various charts and graphics that students can practice reading.

Write on Track Program Guide
- A teaching unit (lesson plans, blackline masters, and additional minilessons) can be found in the Program Guide ring binder.

Reading New Words

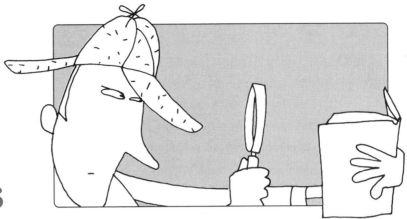

(See handbook pages 200-201.)

Words are the building blocks of reading and writing. To learn to read and write, children need to recognize and spell the most common words quickly and automatically. They also need to develop strategies for recognizing "hard words" that, at first, they cannot pronounce.

Rationale
- Word recognition is an important part of the comprehension process.
- Students need strategies to read new words.

Major Concepts
- **Students can use the "read-and-check" strategy to read new words.** (page 200)
- **Looking for *smaller words* and *common patterns* within "difficult" words is useful.** (page 201)
- **Recognizing and using prefixes, suffixes, and roots to break a long word into smaller parts is also useful.** (page 201)
- **Applying syllable breaks is useful for reading new words.** (page 201)
- **Looking for compound words is another strategy to simplify reading longer words.** (page 201)

Performance Standards

Students are expected to . . .
- read and present information in various forms.
- read and spell prefixes, suffixes, roots, compound words, and syllable constructions correctly.

Getting Started with "Reading New Words"

Start-Up Activity: Write the following sentences on the chalkboard and read them with your students:

> Poinsettia leaves are <u>toxic</u>.
>
> Dogs and cats are <u>quadrupeds</u>.
>
> A lone <u>petrel</u> circled above the boat.

Then have students look at pages 200-201 in their handbooks. Ask them which one (or more) of the strategies might help them read and understand the underlined words. (You might also refer them to the lists of prefixes, suffixes, and roots beginning on page 218.)

Enrichment Activity: Ask pairs or small groups of students to search their social studies or science book for words that have prefixes and suffixes. Have each group record these words, underline the prefixes and suffixes, and write appropriate definitions. Then let each group share their words and definitions with the class.

Teaching Resources

Write on Track Teacher's Guide

- Minilesson:

    "Working on New Words" (page 225)

Write on Track Handbook

- "Building Vocabulary Skills," pages 209-215, and "Using Prefixes, Suffixes, Roots," pages 216-225, provide helpful tools for reading new words.

Write on Track Program Guide

- A teaching unit (lesson plans, blackline masters, and additional minilessons) can be found in the Program Guide ring binder.

Reading to Understand

(See handbook pages 202-207.)

Reading comprehension is the process of making meaning from a text. It is a complex and interactive process—involving the readers' abilities to build upon their own knowledge and skills when they meet new concepts and information. In a sense, the more students know before they read, the more they will be able to understand when they read. Strengthening reading comprehension involves building background knowledge about the concepts that students will encounter in their reading.

Rationale
- Students need strategies to help them become more active and thoughtful readers.
- Students in the middle elementary grades need ways to unlock the structure of informational texts, which are often introduced at this time.
- Many students are capable readers, but, at times, they may not be reading efficiently. For example, they may spend too much time decoding proper nouns, or neglect varying their reading speed.

Major Concepts
- **To read is to understand, learn, remember, and discover.** (page 202)
- **There are several ways students can improve their reading.** (page 202)
- **Reading strategies lead to effective, efficient reading.** (page 203)
- **Reading strategies can be modeled/taught/learned in the context of classroom reading instruction.** (pages 203-207)

Performance Standards
Students are expected to . . .
- exhibit careful reading and understanding of a text.

Getting Started with "Reading to Understand"

Start-Up Activity: Ask students who enjoy reading to share experiences and times they have relished a book. Assure those students who are reluctant or indifferent readers that they could change their feelings about reading if they find a book (or books) that truly interests them. (Many students become avid readers later in their school years!)

Enrichment Activity: Promote interdisciplinary "reading for meaning" by creating a question box in your classroom. Encourage students to submit questions related to their reading in any content area. From time to time, review and discuss these questions. Some of the questions may become the focus of further reading and writing projects for students.

Teaching Resources

Write on Track Teacher's Guide

- Minilessons:
  "Smelly Skunks" (page 225)
  "Mapping" (page 225)

Write on Track Handbook

- "Collection Chart," page 118, offers helpful suggestions for reading and understanding both fiction and nonfiction books.

Write on Track Program Guide

- A teaching unit (lesson plans, blackline masters, and additional minilessons) can be found in the Program Guide ring binder.

Building Vocabulary Skills

(See handbook pages 209-215.)

Students need a strong vocabulary to understand what they read and hear, and to express themselves in writing and speaking. The good news is that children have been learning new words almost since they were born.

Rationale
- A strong vocabulary is fundamental to all language skills.
- Giving students several ways to learn new words equips them with the tools they need to build a strong vocabulary.
- Giving students a variety of word-learning strategies encourages them to be independent learners.

Major Concepts
- **The more words students know, the better they can express their thoughts and feelings.** (page 209)
- **The best way to learn new words is to read a lot.** (page 210)
- **Nearby words can help students figure out new words; keeping track of and using the new words will increase their vocabulary.** (pages 210-211)
- **Dictionaries and thesauruses can help students learn new words.** (pages 212-214)
- **Dividing a word into parts (prefixes, suffixes, roots) can help students understand what the word means.** (page 215)

Performance Standards
Students are expected to . . .
- increase their vocabularies, using a variety of strategies.

Getting Started with "Building Vocabulary Skills"

Start-Up Activity: On an overhead or a chalkboard, write a sentence from a source the students are currently reading. (The line should contain one challenging word.) Mention that everyone sees and hears new words all the time. Encourage students to have a special place in their journals or notebooks to keep a list of new words.

Enrichment Activity: Have students use dictionaries or a Web site to learn the histories of the names of days of the week or months of the year. (Make sure the dictionaries include word histories.) One approach is to have each student look up the month in which he or she was born. Have students write short paragraphs telling what they learned.

Teaching Resources

Write on Track Teacher's Guide

- Minilessons:

  "Word Search" (page 225)

  "Just the Right Word" (page 226)

Write on Track Handbook

- "Using Prefixes, Suffixes, Roots," pages 216-225, is a helpful resource for students seeking to build their vocabularies.

Write on Track Program Guide

- A teaching unit (lesson plans, blackline masters, and additional minilessons) can be found in the Program Guide ring binder.

Using Prefixes, Suffixes, Roots

(See handbook pages 216-225.)

Vocabulary building is a key element in a student's growth as a reader and as an independent learner. Research has shown that memorization of vocabulary lists is an inefficient and inadequate method for enriching vocabulary. What *does* work is to tap into a student's natural curiosity about language.

Rationale
- Vocabulary knowledge is fundamental to reading comprehension.
- Becoming aware of and understanding the meanings of word parts (prefixes, suffixes, and roots) helps students figure out the meanings of new words.

Major Concepts
- **Prefixes are word parts that come at the beginning of a word, before the root.** (pages 217-218)
- **Suffixes are word parts that come at the end of a word, after the root.** (pages 219-220)
- **A root is the main part of a word and helps reveal the word's meaning.** (pages 221-225)

Performance Standards
Students are expected to . . .
- spell and use roots, prefixes, and suffixes correctly.

Getting Started with "Using Prefixes, Suffixes, Roots"

Start-Up Activity: Write *bicycle, tricycle,* and *unicycle* on the board. Ask students how many wheels each one has, and what part of the word tells this. Think of other words that begin with the prefixes *bi, tri,* and *uni.* Also talk about other numerical prefixes, such as *oct* (eight) and *dec* (ten).

Enrichment Activity: For an extended activity, introduce one or two prefixes, suffixes, or roots to study each week. Students could be asked to do the following:

- Think of or find words that contain these word parts; then use these words in sentences.
- Brainstorm for sayings or word associations that could help you remember the word parts.
- Create "new" words using different word parts. (The new words must make sense!)

Teaching Resources

Write on Track Teacher's Guide

- Minilesson:
  "*Un*-lock-*ed*" (page 226)

Write on Track Handbook

- "Building Vocabulary Skills," pages 209-215, offers other helpful vocabulary-building resources.

Write on Track Program Guide

- A teaching unit (lesson plans, blackline masters, and additional minilessons) can be found in the Program Guide ring binder.

Becoming a Better Speller

(See handbook pages 226-229.)

There are many ways for students to acquire a bank of correctly spelled words, including learning to use strategies and basic spelling rules, making a spelling dictionary, and proofreading carefully. Correct spelling, however, should not be an end in itself. The ideal situation for learning to spell well is in the context of reading and writing assignments. Ultimately, it is important for students to realize that correct spelling aids the readability of their work.

Rationale

- Spelling is an important part of the writing and communicating process.
- Students learn to spell as they read and write, not just when they take spelling tests.
- The more experience students have with words, the better spellers they will be.

Major Concepts

- **Many "new" words are related to words students already know how to spell.** (page 226)
- **There are strategies students can use to become better spellers.** (pages 227-228)
- **It helps to use all of the senses when learning to spell.** (page 227)
- **Knowing a few basic rules can help students avoid common errors.** (pages 228-229)

Performance Standards

Students are expected to . . .
- spell accurately in final drafts.
- write with more proficient spelling of regularly spelled patterns and homophones.
- use resources to find correct spellings.

Getting Started with "Becoming a Better Speller"

Start-Up Activity: Have students turn to page 226 in the handbook and read the first paragraph together. Then have them brainstorm for words that contain the base word *light* (*lightning, sunlight, moonlight, highlight, lighter, lights, lighting, twilight, lightly*). Talk about the fact that knowing the word *light* makes it easier to spell all the other words.

Enrichment Activity: When students are proofreading their writing, ask them to circle two to four words that they think may be misspelled. Then have them check and correct these words before they write a final draft. (Have students use personal spelling dictionaries to keep track of words they continue to misspell.)

Teaching Resources

Write on Track Teacher's Guide
- Minilessons:
  "First Cousins" (page 226)
  "By the Rules" (page 226)

Write on Track Handbook
- "Keep a new-word notebook," page 211, gives suggestions for keeping a personal list of words and their meanings.
- "Checking Your Spelling," pages 312-315, provides a list of high-frequency words.
- "Using the Right Word," pages 316-321, provides a list of homophones and other words that can be confused for one another.

Write on Track Program Guide
- A teaching unit (lesson plans, blackline masters, and additional minilessons) can be found in the Program Guide ring binder.

Learning to View

(See handbook pages 231-235.)

Television and the World Wide Web play a major role in shaping what children know and believe about their world. Some students spend as much time watching TV as they do in school! Students are also spending more time on the World Wide Web. This means that children need to become educated viewers of both media.

Rationale
- Students need to become critical viewers of TV and the Web.
- Students will learn more from TV specials if they follow a few active-viewing guidelines.

Major Concepts
- **Some TV programs and Web sites are worthwhile, while others are not worth viewing.** (page 231)
- **Even though TV news doesn't show everything that happens, it should give all the basic facts for events it covers.** (page 232)
- **Students can learn a lot from TV specials by viewing them thoughtfully and actively.** (page 233)
- **TV and Web advertisements have one goal: to get people to buy things. They use many special techniques to accomplish this goal.** (page 234)
- **Students can learn how to decide whether a Web site is trustworthy.** (page 235)

Performance Standards
Students are expected to . . .
- use effective viewing as a tool for learning.

Getting Started with "Learning to View"

Start-Up Activity: Have a class discussion about what programs students watched on TV last evening. Did they like them, or not? What did students learn from their viewing? What confused or bothered them? Talk about the difference between real-life and pretend shows, and try to help students tell them apart.

Enrichment Activity: Have pairs of students create and act out short, simple TV commercials. Each pair should choose a product (real or made-up) and one of the selling methods explained on page 234 in the handbook. Have partners act out their commercials and let the rest of the class identify the selling method being used.

Teaching Resources

Write on Track Teacher's Guide

* Minilesson:

  "Seeing the World" (page 227)

Write on Track Handbook

* "Thinking Clearly," pages 268-273, helps students learn how to evaluate news stories, commercials, and TV specials.
* "Learning to Listen," pages 236-237, reminds students how to be thoughtful listeners, whether they are watching a person or a program.

Write on Track Program Guide

* A teaching unit (lesson plans, blackline masters, and additional minilessons) can be found in the Program Guide ring binder.

Learning to Listen

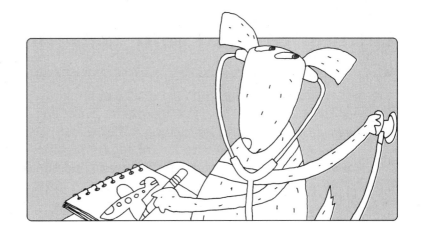

(See handbook pages 236-237.)

Students spend more time listening than they do speaking, reading, and writing combined. With that much "practice," you might expect students to develop good listening skills automatically. But, of course, they don't. Students become good listeners by working at it.

Rationale

- Many students are unaware of the difference between hearing and listening.
- Good listening skills help students learn more and learn faster.
- Good listening skills help students become more successful, not only in the classroom, but also in their personal relationships and in their lives outside of school.

Major Concepts

- **Listening is different from hearing; it involves paying attention and thinking about what is being said.** (page 236)
- **Listening is a learning skill; the better a student listens, the more he or she will learn.** (page 236)
- **Good listeners use their eyes as well as their ears.** (page 237)
- **Good listeners are active listeners. They listen for key words, ask questions, and take notes.** (page 237)

Performance Standards

Students are expected to . . .
- use listening effectively as a tool for learning.

Getting Started with "Learning to Listen"

Start-Up Activity: Ask students to listen as you read the following paragraph.

Children in Australia eat a special birthday treat called "hundreds and thousands" sandwiches. Here's how to make them: First, cut the crusts off some pieces of bread. Second, spread butter on the bread. Third, cut each piece of bread into triangles. Fourth, sprinkle the triangles with lots of sugar sprinkles, called "hundreds and thousands" in all different colors. You've got "hundreds and thousands" sandwiches!

Then ask the following questions. Tell students to raise their hands, but not say anything, if they know the answer to a question. Then call on an individual for each answer.

1. What is the name of the treat you just heard about?
2. In what country is this treat eaten?
3. On what special occasion do people eat this treat?
4. How many steps are there in the recipe?

Tell students that if they learn to listen better, they will learn more.

Enrichment Activity: After studying the chapter on listening, read the directions for making "hundreds and thousands" sandwiches again. Then ask the same questions you asked in the start-up activity. Because students have heard the directions twice, they may be able to answer more complicated questions, such as "What are the four steps you follow to make the treat?" "How do you think this treat got its name?" ("Hundreds and thousands" is the Australian name for sugar sprinkles.)

Teaching Resources

Write on Track Teacher's Guide

- Minilesson:
  "Storytelling" (page 227)

Write on Track Handbook

- "Working with Partners," pages 46-49, offers tips for listening and responding to classmates' writing.
- "Working in Pairs," page 281, lists additional tips for students working together.

Write on Track Program Guide

- A teaching unit (lesson plans, blackline masters, and additional minilessons) can be found in the Program Guide ring binder.

Performing Poems

(See handbook pages 238-243.)

When poetry moves from the page to the stage, we call it poetry performance. Students get on their feet, individually and in teams, to present poetry on stage or in an open space.

Rationale
- To bring poetry to life, children read, hear, and speak poetry.
- Performance encourages cooperative learning.
- Presenting poems gives students a sense of purpose.
- As students take their performance elsewhere, they learn how to conduct themselves in front of groups.

Major Concepts
- **Poetry performance is fun.** (page 238)
- **Many poems can be scripted and scored.** (pages 239-241)
- **Here are five tips for performing poems: act confident, face your audience, name the poem, use an "outside" voice, and exit quietly.** (pages 242-243)

Performance Standards
Students are expected to . . .
- become aware of the power of language in poetry.

Getting Started with "Performing Poems"

Start-Up Activity: Ask students to think of songs and rhymes they know that have movements (such as "Miss Mary Mack," "Heads, Shoulders, Knees and Toes," and "The Eensy Weensy Spider"). Ask individuals or pairs of students to act out some of these rhymes. Explain that performing poems is a similar activity except that students get to make up the movements.

Enrichment Activity: Students who enjoy performing poems may want to try pantomime. Let them make up movements to act out a poem or scene from a story, without speaking. Music, sound effects, costumes, and props could add a special touch. See how well the audience can guess what is being portrayed.

Teaching Resources

Write on Track Teacher's Guide

- Minilesson:

  "Speaking Parts" (page 227)

Write on Track Handbook

- "Writing Free-Verse Poetry," pages 167-173, and "Traditional and Playful Poems," pages 174-179, help students to write poems, which they may then script and perform.

- "Working in Groups," pages 280-283, presents the skills students need to work together to perform their poems.

Write on Track Program Guide

- A teaching unit (lesson plans, blackline masters, and additional minilessons) can be found in the Program Guide ring binder.

Giving Short Talks

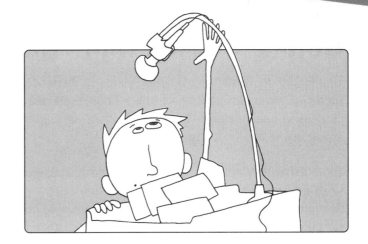

(See handbook pages 244-251.)

Learning to give a short talk will help young students become more comfortable with public speaking—a lifelong skill. In this chapter, students will have the opportunity to prepare and present short talks. They will also be introduced to presenting their talks as multimedia presentations.

Rationale
- Practice in public speaking develops a lifelong skill.
- Preparing and presenting a talk step-by-step teaches students that big assignments are easier when they are divided into smaller tasks.
- Students reinforce skills (such as choosing a topic and gathering information) used in other assignments.

Major Concepts
- **Speaking in front of a group becomes easier with practice.** (page 244)
- **Preparing and giving a short talk can be divided into seven steps.** (pages 245-248)
- **A talk can be "dressed up" with pictures and by preparing a multimedia presentation.** (pages 250-251)

Performance Standards

Students are expected to . . .
- demonstrate oral presentation skills.
- present information in various forms using available technology.

Getting Started with "Giving Short Talks"

Start-Up Activity: Have each student write down a favorite short joke. (Provide joke books for those who can't think of one.) Then have students, one at a time, come to the front of the class and read or tell their jokes. This icebreaker will help students feel more at ease with speaking in front of their classmates.

Enrichment Activity: Have students prepare and give a multimedia computer presentation with their short talks. Follow the guidelines on pages 250-251 in the handbook. Also give students the opportunity to view the multimedia presentation of the sample short talk "Skunks" on page 249. You can access this by visiting <www.thewritesource.com/mm.htm>.

Teaching Resources

Write on Track Teacher's Guide
*   Minilesson:
    "Talk Topic" (page 227)

Write on Track Handbook
*   "Learning to Listen," pages 236-237, helps students to become a good audience for classmates' talks.

Write on Track Program Guide
*   A teaching unit (lesson plans, blackline masters, and additional minilessons) can be found in the Program Guide ring binder.

Learning to Interview

(See handbook pages 252-255.)

Interviewing gets students actively involved in the information-gathering process. When students conduct interviews, they are practicing very important skills: getting organized, speaking, listening, note taking, and thinking clearly.

Rationale
- Conducting an interview shows students that the spoken word can be a valuable source of information and learning.
- The interview process helps students develop listening and speaking skills.

Major Concepts
- **An interview is a way to gather information.** (page 252)
- **Students need to carefully plan and prepare for an interview.** (page 253)
- **Students need to be polite and alert during the interview.** (page 254)
- **Information from an interview can be shared in an interesting talk or report.** (pages 254-255)

Performance Standards
Students are expected to . . .
- use listening effectively as a tool for learning.
- construct questions about a subject.
- take simple notes from oral or tape-recorded interviews.

Getting Started with "Learning to Interview"

Start-Up Activity: Ask students to recall what it's like on the first day of each new school year. Everyone is in a new classroom with a new teacher and at least some new classmates. How do students find out about one another? They ask questions, such as "What's your name?" "Who was your teacher last year?" "Are you new at this school?" "Where did you come from?"

These questions represent an informal interview to gather information. Have students brainstorm for other situations in which they conduct informal interviews, or are "interviewed" by others.

Enrichment Activity: Have each student interview an older person on the general subject of how life was different when that person was the child's age. Students should come up with their own questions. Afterward, have them write paragraphs based on their interviews. Share the results with the class.

Teaching Resources

Write on Track Teacher's Guide
- Minilesson:
  "Dream Job" (page 228)

Write on Track Handbook
- "Learning to Listen," pages 236-237, helps students to become good listeners during an interview.

Write on Track Program Guide
- A teaching unit (lesson plans, blackline masters, and additional minilessons) can be found in the Program Guide ring binder.

Telling Stories

(See handbook pages 256-261.)

Storytelling is as old as society itself. People from around the world have always told tales to pass down their beliefs, history, and traditions to future generations. Telling stories is one of the most fundamental ways to make sense of the world and our place in it.

Rationale
- By sharing stories, children begin to develop a better understanding of themselves, their families, and their world.
- Telling stories improves self-esteem and builds confidence and poise for speaking in front of a group.
- Teaching students how to tell stories provides an outlet for their creative imaginations.
- Storytelling gives the memorization process a purpose.
- As students support one another's efforts, storytelling improves class cooperation.

Major Concepts
- **Telling stories is an age-old tradition.** (page 256)
- **Folktales, fairy tales, legends, and tall tales are all fun to tell.** (page 257)
- **Students can learn to tell stories using a three-step process.** (page 257)

Performance Standards
Students are expected to . . .
- share oral stories with classmates and others.

Getting Started with "Telling Stories"

Start-Up Activity: Point out that people have always told stories. Movies are one way people tell stories today. Have students tell about a favorite part of a movie they have seen, or a special episode of a TV program. (It is often easier to tell a story after seeing it as a movie or TV program.)

Tell students that being a good storyteller is a little like being a moviemaker. Storytellers, like moviemakers, bring stories to life. They use sound effects, different voices, changes in volume, exaggeration, and a variable pace. Telling stories can be fun.

Enrichment Activity: Have students choose a personal narrative or family story they have written, and then adapt it for telling. Encourage them to use good storytelling techniques, including exaggeration, repeated words, sound effects, pacing, and so on. Have students share their stories with small groups or with the whole class.

Teaching Resources

Write on Track Teacher's Guide

- Minilesson:

  "Story Cards" (page 228)

Write on Track Handbook

- "Score the poem," page 241, could serve as a helpful resource as students prepare to tell a story.

- "Performance Tips," page 242, offers guidelines suitable for any oral presentation.

Write on Track Program Guide

- A teaching unit (lesson plans, blackline masters, and additional minilessons) can be found in the Program Guide ring binder.

Using Graphic Organizers

(See handbook pages 263-267.)

Everyone would agree that helping students collect, arrange, and use information is a primary goal of education. The challenge, of course, is how to help them do this. Among other things, students can be introduced to using graphic organizers as a writing-to-learn technique.

Rationale
- Graphic organizers help students organize thoughts and information.
- Students need to practice using graphic organizers for gathering and remembering details, getting facts straight, and arranging information.

Major Concepts
- **Being organized is a key to success.** (page 263)
- **Graphic organizers help learners gather and group ideas.** (page 263)
- **Different graphic organizers serve different purposes.** (pages 263-267)

Performance Standards

Students are expected to . . .
- collect information about a subject.
- use strategies, such as graphic organizers, to generate and organize ideas.

Getting Started with "Using Graphic Organizers"

Start-Up Activity: Have students brainstorm a list of tasks and details that would need to be accomplished for a class trip or holiday celebration. When the list is finished, ask students for ideas about organizing the details, such as sorting by the five senses or the 5 W's. Talk about why it is helpful to organize details.

Enrichment Activity: Show students the time line on pages 382-391 in the handbook. Explain that students can use time lines to show the order of events in history, in a science project, or in a story. Have them make a time line for the events in a story they have read. (Ask them to number the events, as well as assign a time: for example, (1) Early one morning . . . , (2) That night . . . , and so on.) They may use words, pictures, or both to show the events.

Teaching Resources

Write on Track Teacher's Guide

- Minilesson:
  "Circling Around Subjects" (page 228)

Write on Track Handbook

- "Gathering Details," pages 36-37, shows students graphic organizers "at work."
- "Reading to Understand," pages 202-207, presents additional organizers for students' use.

Write on Track Program Guide

- A teaching unit (lesson plans, blackline masters, and additional minilessons) can be found in the Program Guide ring binder.

Thinking Clearly

(See handbook pages 268-273.)

Thinking clearly helps people succeed. It helps attorneys present convincing cases and mechanics repair engines. It helps coaches plan effective strategies for upcoming games and young learners become more successful in almost everything they do—inside and outside of school.

Rationale
- Students need to learn the thinking skills required to solve problems and make decisions.
- Students need to understand the difference between facts and opinions.
- Students need to know how to use facts and opinions correctly in their writing and speaking, and to be aware of how others use facts and opinions.

Major Concepts
- **Thinking clearly is a skill that students can learn.** (page 268)
- **Students can learn to solve problems, step-by-step.** (page 269)
- **Students can use clear thinking to help them make decisions.** (page 270)
- **It's important to understand the difference between facts and opinions.** (pages 271-273)

Performance Standards
Students are expected to . . .
- use effective thinking skills and strategies.

© Great Source. All rights reserved.

Getting Started with "Thinking Clearly"

Start-Up Activity: Ask students to think of a time when they may have gotten lost. Have them discuss how they felt, what they did, why they did it, and how things worked out. What did they learn about how to solve this kind of problem? Then discuss the problem-solving process outlined in the handbook on page 269. Have students compare this process to their own.

Enrichment Activity: Have students identify and evaluate the problem-solving strategies used by characters in one or more stories they have read recently. Ask questions, such as "What was the main character's problem?" "Did the main character think clearly before he or she acted?" "How did things turn out?" "What else could he or she have done?"

As an extension, students can rewrite a story's ending, telling what might have happened if the character had tried a different solution.

Teaching Resources

Write on Track Teacher's Guide
- Minilesson:

   "Trouble, Trouble" (page 228)

Write on Track Handbook
- "Persuasive Paragraph," page 63, uses facts and opinions to convince someone of something.
- "A Letter to Solve a Problem," page 132, demonstrates one practical application for thinking clearly to solve a problem.

Write on Track Program Guide
- A teaching unit (lesson plans, blackline masters, and additional minilessons) can be found in the Program Guide ring binder.

Writing to Learn

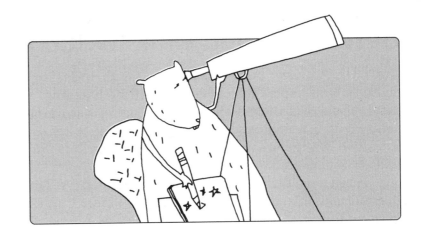

(See handbook pages 274-275.)

There are many connections between writing and learning. When students write about a subject, they can discover new things and reinforce what they already know about the subject. In a sense, writing is like thinking on paper (or on a computer screen).

Rationale
- Writing is an important part of learning.
- Writing reflectively in a learning log broadens students' understanding of concepts, helping them identify and reinforce what they know.

Major Concepts
- **In learning logs, students can record what they do day by day, what they have learned, and any questions they have.**
(pages 274-275)
- **Students can choose from a variety of writing-to-learn strategies.**
(page 275)

Performance Standards

Students are expected to . . .
- use writing as a tool for learning.

Getting Started with "Writing to Learn"

Start-Up Activity: Ask students to clear their desktops of all materials, including pencils, markers, and paper. Tell them they will be listening, but are not allowed to write or take notes. Then read them a slightly challenging word problem (math or riddle) that most students could solve on paper. Give students time to realize that their first response is to want to write down the problem, because this makes it so much easier to solve. This demonstrates that writing is a powerful tool for learning.

After some discussion, read the problem again. This time, allow students to write down the information and solve the problem. Tell them that they will be learning more ways to use "writing to learn."

Enrichment Activity: Assign students to read a short section of their social studies book, describing a machine or process that is important to them. Then have them write a learning-log entry, including simple drawings, to explain what they learned.

Teaching Resources

Write on Track Teacher's Guide
- Minilesson:

  "Logging It" (page 229)

Write on Track Handbook
- "Writing in Journals," pages 77-79, gives a personal slant to writing and learning.

Write on Track Program Guide
- A teaching unit (lesson plans, blackline masters, and additional minilessons) can be found in the Program Guide ring binder.

Completing Assignments

(See handbook pages 277-279.)

Learning to complete assignments means learning to plan ahead. Mastering this skill will enable students to break big tasks into manageable parts, learn from their assignments, and do their best work.

Rationale
- Learning to plan their time and complete long-range assignments is a valuable lifelong skill for young students.
- Learning to complete assignments gives students a sense of confidence and competence.

Major Concepts
- **Planning ahead is a big part of completing assignments successfully.** (page 277)
- **There are strategies students can use to help them complete their assignments.** (page 278)
- **There are forms students can use to write down their plans for daily assignments and big assignments.** (page 279)

Performance Standards - - - -
Students are expected to . . .
- complete classroom assignments on time.

Getting Started with "Completing Assignments"

Start-Up Activity: Have each student write down the names and telephone numbers of two classmates who will be their "homework buddies." Tell students they can call their homework buddies when they miss a day of school, or if they don't understand an assignment. (Have students clear this with their parents.)

Enrichment Activity: Have students work in pairs to make a one-week plan for an out-of-class assignment that includes conducting an interview for a news story, or gathering information for a classroom report. (You may want to give students blank calendars or have them make their own schedules or grids.)

Teaching Resources

Write on Track Teacher's Guide
* Minilesson:
  "Working Smart" (page 229)

Write on Track Handbook
* "Reading to Understand," pages 202-207, provides students with ways to complete their reading assignments effectively and efficiently.

Write on Track Program Guide
* A teaching unit (lesson plans, blackline masters, and additional minilessons) can be found in the Program Guide ring binder.

Working in Groups

(See handbook pages 280-283.)

Some things can only be accomplished by students working together—putting on a play, for example. And some things, although accessible to individuals, are better learned when working with others—such as the multiplication table, for example. Students, however, do need a few basic skills to work with others successfully.

Rationale
- Working in groups allows students to do things they could not do alone.
- Knowing how to work as a member of a group is an important lifelong skill.
- Students need to learn basic teamwork skills, such as listening, sharing, and compromising.

Major Concepts
- **Some things can only be accomplished by people working together in groups.** (page 280)
- **Two people who work together are called partners.** (page 281)
- **Working in a group requires listening to others and sharing ideas and jobs.** (page 282)
- **Every group project should include a plan.** (page 283)

Performance Standards

Students are expected to . . .
- learn basic teamwork skills.

Getting Started with "Working in Groups"

Start-Up Activity: Have students, individually, list things they would need to take if they were going camping in the wilderness or visiting another planet. Then have students, in pairs, combine their lists, deleting duplicates. Did any individuals forget something important that their partners thought of? Finally, on the board, make a list that compiles the lists from at least three or four pairs. Did any pairs forget something important that other pairs thought of? Point out how the list gets better as more students contribute to it.

Enrichment Activity: When students have finished studying a chapter or unit in social studies or science, have them work in small groups to make booklets for younger readers. The booklets could use simple text, and, after they are edited, a variety of visuals (drawings, graphics, maps, photographs, and so on) could be added. If possible, give students opportunities to share their booklets with younger students.

Teaching Resources

Write on Track Teacher's Guide
- Minilesson:
  "Surprise!" (page 229)

Write on Track Handbook
- "Working with Partners," pages 46-49, covers the skills needed in effective writing groups.

Write on Track Program Guide
- A teaching unit (lesson plans, blackline masters, and additional minilessons) can be found in the Program Guide ring binder.

Taking Tests

(See handbook pages 284-291.)

Tests are an inescapable part of school, and, for some, not always a pleasant part. Yet tests are an important way for both teachers and students to assess how they are doing.

Rationale
- Tests are one way to measure learning about a subject.
- Understanding how to prepare for and take various kinds of tests can empower students.

Major Concepts
- **Tests are not a problem if students study and keep up with their class work.** (page 284)
- **There are things students can do to prepare for any kind of test.** (page 285)
- **There are strategies students can use to do their best on objective and short-answer tests.** (pages 286-289)
- **There are tips students can follow to answer a writing prompt and to remember facts for a test.** (pages 290-291)

Performance Standards - - - - -

Students are expected to . . .
- demonstrate an understanding of what they are learning.

Getting Started with "Taking Tests"

Start-Up Activity: Let students have some fun expressing their feelings about tests. Have them "draw their answers" to this question: If a test were an animal, what kind of animal would it be? (Remind them what a caption is, and have them write simple captions for their drawings.)

Enrichment Activity: Have each student make a "Taking-Tests Checklist." Instruct students to review a topic they are studying and list the ideas and tips they think will help them remember this information. (You may want to have them use the checklists in the handbook as models.)

Teaching Resources

Write on Track Teacher's Guide

- Minilesson:
  "Short Answer" (page 229)

Write on Track Handbook

- "Expository Paragraph," page 62, and "Persuasive Paragraph," page 63, provide basic guidelines that will help students respond to writing prompts.
- "Thinking Clearly," pages 268-273, helps students develop skills necessary for taking objective tests.

Write on Track Program Guide

- A teaching unit (lesson plans, blackline masters, and additional minilessons) can be found in the Program Guide ring binder.

Proofreader's Guide

Introductory Notes

This section introduces the "Proofreader's Guide" in the handbook and provides getting-started ideas to help you with your initial planning.

	Teacher's Guide	Student Handbook
Marking Punctuation	**151**	**293-303**
Checking Mechanics		**304-311**
Checking Your Spelling		**312-315**
Using the Right Word		**316-321**
Understanding Sentences		**322-325**
Understanding Our Language		**326-337**

Proofreader's Guide

(See handbook pages 292-337.)

The "Proofreader's Guide" is a student resource for learning about the skills of language. This section, noteworthy for its yellow pages, is easy to find and easy to use for young student writers. The yellow pages are close to the end of the book, emphasizing that checking proofreading for errors in writing is close to the end of the writing process.

Rationale
- Students learn to improve their writing through developing their editing and proofreading skills.
- Students learn to use a handbook as a reference tool.

Major Concepts
- **"Marking Punctuation" and "Checking Mechanics" cover the information students need to know about punctuation, capitalization, plurals, numbers, and abbreviations.** (pages 293-311)
- **"Checking Your Spelling" and "Using the Right Word" include high frequency words that students regularly use in their writing.** (pages 312-321)
- **"Understanding Sentences" and "Understanding Our Language" help students learn about sentences and the parts of speech.** (pages 322-337)

Performance Standards

Students are expected to . . .
- use standard English to communicate clearly and effectively.
- be able to identify and use the different parts of speech.
- write in complete sentences.
- use punctuation and capitalization correctly.

Getting Started with the "Proofreader's Guide"

Start-Up Activity: Play a search game in which pairs of students hunt for information in the "Proofreader's Guide."

> Go to "Marking Punctuation," beginning on page 293.
>> Write the names of three punctuation marks.
> Go to "Checking Mechanics," beginning on page 304.
>> Write five common abbreviations.
> Go to "Using the Right Word," beginning on page 316.
>> Write a new set of sentences for the words *hear* and *here.*
> Go to "Understanding Our Language," beginning on page 326.
>> Name the eight parts of speech.

Enrichment Activity: Have students make their own spelling booklets or thesauruses, using words of their own choice and words from "Checking Your Spelling" (pages 312-315) and "Using the Right Word" (pages 316-321). Encourage them to use art, sample sentences, or acronyms to reinforce correct spelling.

Teaching Resources

Write on Track Teacher's Guide

- Minilessons:
  Pages 230-237 contain more than 25 minilessons for the "Proofreader's Guide."

Write on Track Handbook

- "Writing Basic Sentences," pages 71-73, includes a review of sentence parts and sentence problems.

Write on Track Program Guide

- A teaching unit (lesson plans, blackline masters, and additional minilessons) can be found in the Program Guide ring binder.

Student Almanac

Introductory Notes

This section introduces the "Student Almanac" in the handbook and provides getting-started ideas to help you with your initial planning.

	Teacher's Guide	Student Handbook
Using Language	155	339-347
Exploring Science		348-353
Improving Math Skills		354-363
Using Maps		364-379
History in the Making		380-391

Student Almanac

(See handbook pages 338-391.)

The "Student Almanac" contains interesting and useful information about language, science, math, maps, and history. Students can use it to answer questions that come up as they work on assignments, and to enrich their writing.

Rationale
- Students learn to use reference materials to answer questions and to improve their writing and other classwork.
- Students practice interpreting visual information as they use the section's many charts.

Major Concepts
- **"Using Language" helps to broaden students' understanding of how language develops, including an essay on the history of English and charts of borrowed words and foreign-language greetings. Sign language, Braille, and handwriting charts are also helpful.** (pages 339-347)
- **"Exploring Science" offers students a variety of information to enrich their writing and other projects with facts about animals, the solar system, and U.S. and metric measurements.** (pages 348-353)
- **"Improving Math Skills" provides strategies for solving word problems, rounding numbers, and telling time. There are also helpful tables of math symbols and facts.** (pages 354-363)
- **"Using Maps" offers a basic guide to map reading, followed by world, U.S., and regional maps. Additional tables show U.S. geographic facts.** (pages 364-379)
- **"History in the Making" presents a U.S. map of early Native American regions and a time line spanning 1492 to 2000.** (pages 380-391)

Performance Standards

Students are expected to . . .
- collect information about a topic.
- take simple notes from relevant sources.

Getting Started with the "Student Almanac"

Start-Up Activity: As a class, go through the almanac page by page. Have students share ideas for using various charts. Encourage them to be creative. For example, the information on our solar system could provide facts for a report. But it could also provide ideas for a fantasy story, a poem, or an alphabet book about space. A student might name the characters in a story after planets, or use one planet as a setting. Combined with the facts about animals, there's no telling what kind of fantasy stories could result. (Monkeys on Mars?)

Enrichment Activity: As a class or in small groups, have students create an additional section for the almanac. First, they must decide on a subject for the section. Remind students that their new section should be both fun to read and helpful. Second, they must decide on the information to be included in the section. Have them brainstorm a list of tables, charts, illustrations, and maps that you will need to create. Third, have students work individually or in pairs to research and create each part of the section. Finally, compile the section and keep it available for students to use.

Teaching Resources

Write on Track Teacher's Guide

- Minilessons:
  Pages 238-244 contain more than 20 minilessons for the "Proofreader's Guide."

Write on Track Handbook

- "The Tools of Learning," pages 180-291, includes "Working in Groups," pages 280-283, as well as many other learning strategies that students will use across the curriculum.

Write on Track Program Guide

- A teaching unit (lesson plans, blackline masters, and additional minilessons) can be found in the Program Guide ring binder.

Writing Programs

The writing programs described on the following pages offer a variety of approaches to meet the individual needs of your students.

Effective Writing Instruction

So much has been written about writing that it is easy today for any teacher to become overwhelmed by all the different writing approaches. No matter which writing approach you choose, remember that all effective writing instruction shares these two goals:

1. Students learn to write.

Students learn to write in the same way all writers learn—by doing. The best writing program gives students frequent, varied, and significant writing opportunities. Writing isn't taught by teacher lectures, prescriptive textbooks, or isolated skill-and-drill exercises. Students need real purposes and real audiences for their writing. Students need meaningful responses to their writing, as well as guidance and specific instruction about their current writing assignments.

2. Students write to learn.

Writing is thinking on paper. Writing lets students explore ideas and questions—about themselves, about the world, about subjects they're studying in school. Students in effective writing programs write to explore, understand, learn, discover, and pass along information.

What are the characteristics of effective writing programs?

Student centered: In strong writing programs, students write rather than listen to a teacher lecture about writing. They experiment with the writing process to discover how writing works for them.

No textbook needed: Most textbooks by their nature are prescriptive. They are designed to teach writing skills, but they are also intended to tie the teacher and student to the textbook. Good writing programs encourage independent thinking and use the students' own writing as the text.

Individualized: Because all writers are unique, one formula for writing doesn't work for all students at the same time. Strong writing programs allow students to write and work individually. The teacher provides assistance and instruction as it is needed.

Interactive classroom structure: Strong writing programs promote active learning. Writing classrooms are structured to reflect real writing experiences. Students interact with each other and with the teacher to discuss their writing. There's no hiding in the last row of the classroom as the teacher lectures.

Adaptable and integrated curriculum: A good writing program is open to improvement. It must be flexible enough to accommodate new methods of writing instruction or assessment. If an existing method or routine doesn't work with a particular group of students, changes are made. In addition, a good writing program combines various approaches to provide the best writing opportunities for the students.

An Overview of the Approaches

As you search for an appropriate writing approach, you will see that these five approaches can be combined. For example, the thematic approach incorporates the process approach and the writing-workshop approach, and could include the trait-based approach. So consider an approach (or a combination) that best fits the needs of your students.

1 Process Approach

While using this approach, students learn that writing—real writing—is a process of exploration and discovery rather than an end product. As students develop their writing, they use all the steps in the writing process—prewriting, drafting, revising, editing and proofreading, and publishing. And the writing they develop, for the most part, stems from their own thinking.

Write on Track discusses the writing process (beginning on page 11). Guidelines for the specific forms of writing are also organized according to the steps in the writing process. (See pages 160-161 in this guide for more on the writing process.)

2 Thematic Approach

When using this approach, the teacher (with student input) chooses a theme that serves as the focal point for an experience that immerses students in a variety of integrated reading, writing, and speaking activities. Writing projects evolve from these activities. (See page 162 in this guide for more on the thematic approach.)

3 Personal Experience Approach

In this approach students enjoy writing and find it meaningful because it stems from their personal experiences and observations.

Both journal writing and freewriting help students write honestly about their personal experiences when they do assigned writing. These types of writing help students produce writing that readers will find interesting and entertaining.

As students become confident in their personal writing, they become more secure in making their writing public. (See page 163 in this guide for more information.)

4 Trait-Based Approach

Trait-based instruction focuses on key features—or traits—that most writers, editors, and thoughtful readers agree are essential to writing success. A list of these traits follows:

- ✔ interesting ideas
- ✔ clear organization
- ✔ personal voice
- ✔ well-chosen words
- ✔ smooth sentences
- ✔ correct copy

Students are taught each trait individually, but eventually they combine all of them in revising and editing their work. They find examples of each trait in the writing all around them, assessing their own and others' writing for these key features. Trait-based instruction makes writing and revision manageable for students. They may use trait-based rubrics to guide their writing process from start to finish. (See pages 176-180 in this guide for the rubrics and pages 164-165 and 174-175 for more information.)

5 Writing Workshop Approach

In a writing workshop, students write or work on writing-related issues every day (reading, researching, responding, participating in collaborative writing, etc.). They keep all of their writing in folders and produce a specified number of finished pieces each quarter. They are encouraged to experiment with new forms and techniques. Support during each writing project comes from both peer and teacher conferences. Students use the steps in the writing process to develop their writing, and they share their writing in class.

The teacher acts as a facilitator and guide. Desks and chairs are arranged to make student interaction easy, and the classroom is stocked with relevant reading and writing materials. Instruction and advice are given as they are needed on an individual basis, in small groups, or to the entire class. (See page 166 in this guide for more information.)

The Process Approach

What is the "writing process"?

The process approach emphasizes the steps a student goes through while writing. *Write on Track* divides the writing process into these steps: prewriting, writing, revising, editing and proofreading, and publishing.

Before you implement this approach, remember these key points:

- The writing process is not linear; it is cyclical. Steps or stages are repeated in different orders with different writers and different writing assignments.

- The writing process is unique for every writer.

- Not all writing needs to progress through all the steps of the writing process. Sometimes writing will remain in a prewriting form, and sometimes it will progress through the whole process and become a public piece.

How can the process approach be implemented?

- Provide many models of the writing process in action—professional, student, and your own. Write with your students so that you can work through the writing process with them in real ways.

- Be sure that your students understand and can model the stages of the writing process. In addition, help students individualize the steps of the process to best meet their own writing needs.

- Have students create and use writing folders in which to store writing pieces that are "in progress." Choose a method for organizing the folder. Some teachers use separate folders for each piece of writing; others prefer to put all pieces in one large folder.

- Give students many opportunities for practicing the steps of the writing process—learning the writing process takes time.

> " . . . brilliant writers are born. Sure, some are, but it's equally true that brilliant writers can develop over time with lots of practice, opportunities to share their writing with a caring, responsive audience, and focused support from a competent writing teacher."
>
> **—LOIS BRIDGES**

Strategies for Teaching the Steps in the Writing Process

In addition to the prewriting, drafting, revising, editing and proofreading, and publishing strategies offered in *Write on Track,* try these ideas:

Prewriting

Sensory Clusters

Have students use the cluster with a twist—cluster an idea using the five senses. This is a great way to cluster for a descriptive writing piece.

Question Clusters

Have students cluster, focusing on the questions surrounding their topic. Perhaps they could use the 5 W's (who, what, when, where, and why) to develop their cluster ideas.

Freewriting

The world provides a wealth of writing ideas when it is explored through the senses. Have students explore different places, using their senses. For example, have them freewrite after taking a walk outside. Ask them to freewrite after visiting a grocery store, a shopping mall, an airport, or a zoo. Have them refer to these ideas in the future.

Drafting

Do you hear what I am saying?

Put students into small groups (no more than three students per group). Have them talk through their stories or ideas. Ask them to share with the group and have the others in the group respond. What sounds clear? What are they not sure of?

Great Authors, Great Ideas

Read some great beginnings and endings to your students. Try to choose very different styles so that your students don't become convinced that there is only one right way to write an introduction or an ending. Choose examples from their favorite authors, read-alouds, and various forms of writing. Read and discuss together what makes each of these introductions and conclusions work.

Collaborative Authors

Practice writing a draft by working collaboratively as a class to develop an idea with a strong beginning, middle, and ending. Plan out the draft and then write it together as a class.

Teacher Drafters

Share your own draft—not a finished product—with your students. (A letter makes a good sample.) Talk with them about how you worked through the drafting process.

Revising

Scaffolding Sections

If a section such as the introduction is giving students problems, invite them to try a different version. Do the same for conclusions that are giving them problems. If some part of the middle section is causing problems, suggest different ways to include specific details about the topic of the piece.

Teacher Revisers

This activity is a continuation of "Teacher Drafters" (above). Make an overhead of your first draft; discuss the strengths and weaknesses of the draft with your students. Then show your students your revision work, and share a second draft.

Editing and Proofreading

Symbol Alert

Share copyediting symbols and practice using them with students.

Post it!

Make posters of particularly effective sentences, and of common usage problems. Post them in the classroom as an inspiration and a reminder for students.

Publishing

Author's Chair

Donald Graves offers the concept of an "author's chair" as an alternative to traditional publishing. Students may take turns sitting in this specially designated chair to share their completed writing pieces as authentic authors.

School Sharing

Have students share their writing with other students in the school. For example, when exploring writing for different audiences, have students write children's stories and then share the final copy with young students.

What are the results of the writing process?

- Students find writing more meaningful because it becomes a reflection of their own thinking.
- Students develop a feel for writing.
- Students develop independent thinking skills and take pride in their work.
- Students develop a better attitude toward writing, which results in better writing for students of all abilities.

The Thematic Approach

What is the thematic approach?

In the thematic approach to writing, students write to respond to literature or to extend what they are learning in another class. To complete writing projects, students may work individually, in small groups, or as a whole class. Other approaches, such as the writing process approach and the writing workshop approach, are often incorporated into the thematic approach.

Remember these key points:

- Thematic writing provides an avenue for students to write to learn. Choose a theme that students can explore meaningfully.

- Thematic writing units usually take a week or two to complete. During that time, students work for 20-45 minutes daily on their writing project. They work through the steps of the writing process—from prewriting to publishing.

- Students work collaboratively on the thematic writing project. Students help make decisions about the type of writing project, its length, its audience, and the time schedule, as teachers guide them through the writing process.

How can the thematic approach be implemented?

- Students must be familiar with the theme before beginning a thematic writing project. After students have begun a reading selection, or learned some key concepts in a thematic unit, they will likely be ready to begin.

- Thematic projects may be written individually, in small groups, or as a class. Decide which arrangement works best for the theme, your students, and the type of writing you want them to do.

- The thematic writing approach may incorporate the process approach.

Thematic Approach Strategies

Prewriting

Introduce thematic writing projects with opportunities for students to reflect on the theme. For example, for a transportation theme, ask students to help create a list of vehicles that people have used throughout history. Have each student choose one vehicle to research and write about. Read about vehicles and their inventors.

Drafting

Talk with students about possible writing projects for the theme. Offering choices helps students take ownership of their writing. Here are some example projects for the theme of transportation:

- detailed descriptions of their chosen vehicles, including illustrations
- stories about the importance of their vehicles in the lives of people
- journal entries by someone whose vehicle breaks down

Revising

On Your Own ● Use the trait-based approach to have students review and revise their drafts for ideas, organization, and voice.

Writing Groups ● After self-assessment and revision, have students meet together to share their drafts and discuss possible revisions.

Editing and Proofreading

Red Pen Alert! ● Have students proofread their drafts for spelling and punctuation.

Focused Minilessons ● In small groups or with the class, address common problems.

Publishing

Display the transportation writing projects. Have a vehicle celebration. Facilitate improvisations in which student authors take other students on fanciful rides—on everything from a stagecoach to a tall ship to a monorail.

The Personal Experience Approach

What is the personal experience approach?

Personal experience is a natural place for students to begin their writing. With this approach, they explore their thinking, questions, and interests. Developing such personal writing prepares students for more complex, content-oriented writing.

Before you implement this approach, remember these key points:

- Journals, which are the main component of the personal approach, can be used in many different ways to accomplish different goals.
- Students are encouraged to write freely in their personal writing journals, without worrying about grades.
- The audience for this type of writing is often limited—sometimes the writer is the only reader.

How can the personal approach be implemented?

- Establish a classroom environment that invites students to write. Provide stimulating topic ideas through an abundance of resources—books, magazines, posters, displays.
- Write often. Students become more comfortable with writing in journals when they do it often. Establish a classroom routine for journal writing.
- Write for a prescribed period of time. Ask students to write nonstop for 5-10 minutes on a topic. At first this will be difficult, but as students become more comfortable with journal writing, they will be able to write more freely.
- Establish an audience. Will the writing be shared with the teacher? With other students?

Strategies for Implementing the Personal Approach

In addition to the journal-writing strategies provided in the handbook, try these ideas:

Journals for Personal Experiences

The Diary ● In this journal, students record their thoughts. Due to the private nature of this type of writing, it may or may not be shared.

Freewriting Journal ● Teachers direct this journal by offering several prompts that lead students to explore ideas. This journal is used throughout the week for 10-minute quick writes.

Dialogue Journal ● This journal serves as an avenue of communication between teachers and individual student writers. Dialogue may be personal or about a subject area being studied.

Journals for Reactions

Personal Notebook ● In this journal, students record ideas and observations that they may use in future writing projects.

Class or Project Journal ● In this journal, students respond to what is being studied in class or to what they are reading. Questions, predictions, and commentaries are common in this type of journal. Students also use the class or project journal to record progress in a group project.

Journals for Analyses

Learning Log ● Students use this journal to record what they are learning. In science, for example, this could take the form of an observation log for an experiment. In social studies, this could be a freewriting exploring the relationship between what students are learning now and their past experiences or knowledge. In math, a learning log could explain or summarize the math concepts discussed in class.

The Trait-Based Approach

What is the trait-based approach?

The focus of the trait-based approach is helping students identify, in their own writing and in the writing of others, those qualities that make writing strong. This approach doesn't replace other writing approaches. For example, it may rely on the process and the writing workshop approaches.

Before implementing this approach, remember these key points:

- The trait-based approach helps students develop (a) the skills needed to become good assessors of writing and (b) strategies to improve their writing.

- When students understand the traits of good writing, they can assess their own writing, no matter what form it takes.

- Before you can teach the traits, you need to know them yourself. Check the *Write on Track* handbook for more information on the traits (pages 18-21), as well as the section on assessment in this guide (pages 172-180).

How can the trait-based approach be implemented?

- Teach the traits to students by first identifying and discussing the qualities of good writing. After establishing the criteria that you and your students will use to distinguish good writing, explain how each of the traits focuses on a component of good writing.

- Select writing models from various sources: student pieces (with permission), newspaper articles, travel brochures, workplace writing, and so on. Discuss how the traits of effective writing *are* (or *are not*) demonstrated in the models.

- Teach the traits separately, taking time to build student confidence and understanding of each trait. Again, use real models. (See the specific strategies that follow.)

- Create classroom posters that illustrate the traits.

- Use trait language when responding to student writing, and ask students to use trait language when responding to one another's writing.

- As a class, with a student's permission, score his or her writing piece together. Keep refining students' assessment skills.

- Encourage peer-response groups (not peer-editing groups) in which students discuss their writing using the traits of effective writing as the standard.

- Share rubrics (scoring guides) with students before they begin writing so they understand your expectations for each writing task. (See the rubrics on pages 176-180 in this guide.)

Strategies for Teaching the Trait-Based Approach

Trait 1: Interesting Ideas

- Ask students to bring a paragraph from home—from a newspaper, a recipe, an advertisement. As a class or in small groups, discuss whether the information is interesting enough to keep their attention.

- Have students find interesting paragraphs or sections in a reading selection they are familiar with.

Trait 2: Clear Organization

- Have students give detailed directions from their home to school, or have them explain how to do something. Follow up with a discussion of why clear organization is important.

- Read cookbook directions or how-to manuals to see the importance of careful organization.

- Choose a short story with excellent transitions; cut it up into pieces and have small groups of students reassemble the story. Discuss how transitions aid organization.
- Look at the introductions (and conclusions) of some of your students' favorite read-aloud books. Discuss what makes the beginnings and conclusions "work."

Trait 3: Personal Voice

- Have students write an imaginary conversation with themselves. Suggest a situation, such as being alone on a stormy night. Have them write using two different voices—one voice calm and reassuring, the other voice panicked and scared. Share the freewritings and discuss what makes the voices in each of the conversations different.
- Have your students write two sets of recipe directions for the same recipe: one set of directions for a small child, and one for a classmate. Do this activity in small groups and then share the directions. Discuss how the voice varies depending on the audience.
- Together, define "voice" so that all your students understand the concept. Post the definition along with models demonstrating strong voice on a bulletin board.

Trait 4: Well-Chosen Words

- Challenge students to find replacements for overused words. Assign students in small groups to come up with a list of possible words to replace a word such as "said" or "nice." Give students a time limit and then have them share the words they have chosen as replacements.
- Display posters of replacement-word lists to keep the choices visible to the students.
- Study greeting cards and poetry for examples of carefully chosen words.

Trait 5: Smooth Sentences

- Give students two paragraph models: one with very short, choppy sentences and the other with only one long sentence. Ask students to rewrite the paragraphs by changing the sentence lengths, making sentences in the paragraph flow smoothly from one to the next.
- Ask students to read different writing models aloud. Encourage them to read expressively. Discuss how sentence fluency relates to expressive writing and reading.

Trait 6: Correct Copy

- Practice editing skills with pages from the *Write on Track SkillsBook*. Students may work on these activities individually, in small groups, or as a class.
- Have students practice editing skills in small groups by focusing on one skill at a time.
- Have students bring in any error examples they find—from newspapers, business letters, instructions, etc.
- Reward students for finding possible errors in classroom handouts!
- Use student-made posters of copyediting marks in your classroom editing work. (See the inside back cover of *Write on Track* for these marks.)

The Writing Workshop Approach

What is the writing workshop approach?

The writing workshop approach focuses clearly on a way of structuring writing in the classroom. (See the weekly schedule in the next column.) Before you implement this approach, remember these key points:

- This approach establishes a community of writers. Students and teachers work collaboratively through the writing process.
- The atmosphere of classrooms using the writing workshop approach is relaxed—less structured.
- Students write daily for an established period of time with this approach.
- Students work through the steps of the writing process at their own pace, conferring with other students and the teacher when necessary.

How can the writing workshop approach be implemented?

- Though the classroom structure of this approach is relaxed, routines must be established. Setting up a class schedule allows students to anticipate what they will accomplish within a class period.
- To encourage creative writing topics, stock your classroom with interactive, stimulating resources.
- Establish distinct areas within the classroom for tasks: a conference area, an editing and proofreading area, a writing area, and a publishing area.
- Establish your role as facilitator of the writing process. Your role is not to provide all of the ideas for students, but to respond to, discuss, develop, encourage, and even challenge writing ideas provided by students.

Strategies for Implementing the Writing Workshop Approach

See a writing workshop in action by studying the sample schedule below. Here you will see how one teacher organized his writing workshop. This schedule reserves time for minilessons, status checks, individual or group work, and sharing sessions.

Because the schedule is designed for one of the first weeks of a workshop, all students are asked to participate in the minilessons. In time, you can meet the needs of your students by inviting only those attempting certain goals or encountering particular problems to do minilessons. All other students will be actively engaged with a piece of writing or another option you have offered.

Mon.	Tues.	Wed.	Thurs.	Fri.
Writing Minilessons (10 minutes as needed)				
Status Checks (2 minutes) Find out what students will work on for the day.				
Individual Work (30 minutes) Writing, Revising, Editing, Conferencing, or Publishing				
Whole Class Sharing Session (5 minutes)				

Writing Throughout the Day

The writing suggestions offered in this section will help your students use writing as an important learning tool in any content area, whether it is mathematics, science, or language arts.

Writing for Specific Subject Areas   **168**

Writing for Specific Subject Areas

Writing (throughout the day) across the curriculum is the use of writing as a teaching and learning tool in all subject areas. Based on subject matter and learning goals, you choose which writing activities to use and how to use them. The following pages provide specific ways to implement different forms of writing throughout the day. Many of the suggested activities include cross references to related material in the *Write on Track* handbook.

Getting Started

Remember that writing activities can take many forms: graded and nongraded, short and long, school based and personal, revised and edited writing, and writing that never goes beyond a first draft. You will find that these activities will help your students write to learn, and learn to write.

Science

● **Lots of Habitats** Write a classroom report about one animal or plant that is important to one of these habitats: the desert, the woodlands, the ocean, or the rain forest. (See "Writing Classroom Reports," pages 135-141.)

● **Remember to Recycle** Write a letter to your local newspaper, reminding readers about the importance of recycling. (See "Letter to the Editor," page 113.)

● **List it.** Write a list poem about the ocean or the solar system. Perform the poem. (See "A List Poem," page 89, and "Performing Poems," pages 238-243.)

● **New Facts About Food** Write a human-interest story about a person who has made an interesting discovery about nutrition. Or, write a news story about some new food facts. (See "Writing Newspaper Stories," pages 108-113.)

● **I love it here!** Pretend that you are an animal in a desert, a rain forest, an ocean, or a woodland habitat. Then write a personal narrative in which you tell about a day in your life and why you enjoy the place where you live. (See "Writing Personal Narratives," pages 82-85.)

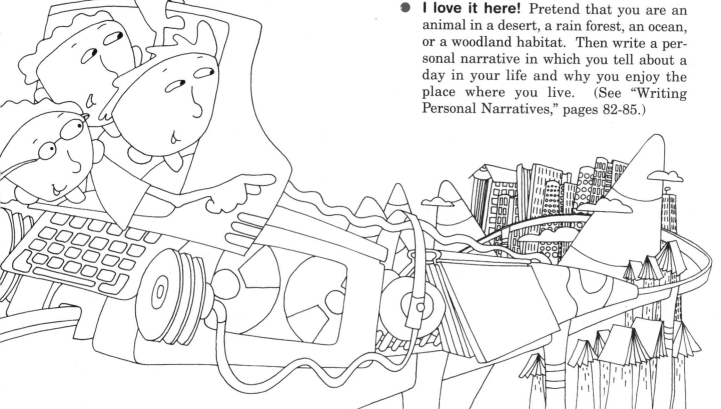

Mathematics

- **Story Problems** Write a story problem about a brother and sister who are doing the dishes. Your problem should include the number of children (2) and the number of dishes (your choice), and it should ask the reader to figure out how to divide the job equally.

- **How-To Divide** Write the steps telling how to fold a piece of paper into eight equal parts. Get a piece of paper and do the activity as you do the writing. (See "How-To Writing," pages 120-125.)

- **Graph it.** For two weeks, keep track of the reading you do outside of school. Make a bar graph. Each bar is a day of the week, and its length shows the number of minutes you spent reading. (You don't have to read every day.) After a month, see if you notice any patterns in your reading habits. (See "Learning About Bar Graphs," page 198.)

- **Sentence Patterns** Choose a story or report that you have written. Count the number of sentences in the whole paper. Then count the number of words in each sentence. Make a graph that shows the length of each sentence. Does your graph show an interesting "roller coaster" of sentence lengths? Keep this in mind as you write future stories and reports. (See "Learning About Bar Graphs," page 198, and "Combining Sentences," pages 74-75.)

- **Story-Problem Machine** Write interesting story problems about life in your home, school, or community. Or, write about imaginary problems ("How many days could an elephant be fed with 550 pounds of hay and 125 gallons of water if an elephant needs 110 pounds of hay and 25 gallons of water a day?"). Solve your problem before you ask your classmates to solve it. (See "Sample Word Problem," page 356.)

> " . . . try to immerse learners in contexts rich in multiple ways of knowing and to invite their inquiry and collaboration."
>
> —B. BERGHOFF, K. EGAWA, J. HARSTE, B. HOONAN

Social Studies

- **Celebration Times** Write a paragraph describing the way your family celebrates a special holiday. Use your senses to write this description. (See "Descriptive Paragraph," page 61.)

- **School Days** Interview an older person in your town and ask them about their school days. Then give a short talk or multimedia presentation comparing the school days of the older person with your own school days. (See "Learning to Interview," pages 252-255, and "Giving Short Talks," pages 244-251.)

- **City Lights** Prepare a photo essay about your city or town. Use photographs or draw pictures for this project. (See "Writing Photo Essays," pages 142-147.)

- **Then and Now** Use a Venn diagram to compare one part of life in colonial times to the same part in present-day times. For instance, compare food and cooking, clothing, heating, transportation, school, entertainment, and so on. Use your completed Venn diagram to write a report about your findings. (See "Comparing Two Subjects," page 266.)

- **Journaling by Candlelight** Select a time in history that you are studying. Decide which historical figure you will be. Write diary entries for one or two days of your life. Write about things that will show how different life was then compared to life today. (See "Writing in Journals," pages 77-79.)

Health/Physical Education

- **ABC Wellness** Make a class alphabet book about wellness topics. Each student in the class could be responsible for one or two letters. For each letter, they should choose a subject related to staying healthy, then write a sentence and draw a picture for that topic.

- **Health Trouble** Write a short play about two healthy characters trying to convince a third character to change an unhealthy habit. If you wish, turn it into a fable by using animal characters. (See "Writing Plays," pages 160-165.)

- **Daily Moves** Write a persuasive paragraph convincing someone that exercise is an important part of staying healthy. Give some tips for possible daily activities—walking, jumping rope, swimming, and so on. (See "Persuasive Paragraph," page 63.)

- **Talking Up Fitness** Prepare a short talk about your favorite exercise. Explain how the body is helped by this exercise and how it keeps you healthy. (See "Giving Short Talks," pages 244-251.)

- **Specialists** There are ophthalmologists, podiatrists, cardiologists, neurologists, and so on. Select one part of the body, and find out the name for a doctor who specializes in that part of the body. Write a paragraph sharing what you learned. (See "Expository Paragraph," page 62.)

Music/Art

- **Introducing . . .** Make an album about a famous artist or musician. (See "Making Albums," pages 80-81.)

- **Laugh Time** Tell a funny story about a pet or a cartoon character; add music to introduce your story. (See "Telling Stories," pages 256-261.)

- **Backdrop** Paint a large mural as the background for a scene that you will use for a class play. (See "Writing Plays," pages 160-165.)

Language Arts

- **Two Ways** Write the nouns for at least 10 things in your classroom. (See "Nouns," page 327.)

- **Nice Adjectives** Write as many words as you can think of that mean the same as the adjective *nice*. You can brainstorm with some classmates and use a thesaurus. (See "Adjectives," pages 333-334.)

- **Answers Please** When you interview someone, you have to ask good questions. Write at least five interrogative sentences (questions) that you would want to ask in an interview with a clown, a bus driver, a dentist, or an artist. (See "Learning to Interview," pages 252-255.)

- **Look and Listen** When students return from a recess break, ask them to write a description of something they saw and heard during recess. Consider the types of things students noticed and how differently they responded to what was happening. Mention that these differences are part of the trait "personal voice." (See "Descriptive Paragraph," page 61.)

- **Two by Two** Ask students to list words that rhyme with the word "tree." Then ask each student to compose a couplet about trees. (See "Rhyme" on page 173 for a model couplet.) Using the couplets, create a class poem about trees.

- **Q and A** Following an oral reading or presentation, ask students to write one question that their classmates should be able to answer, based on the information that was just shared. (See "Good-Listener Checklist" on page 237.)

- **Stop 'n' Write** When you show a video in class, stop the recording at a significant point and ask students to write about what they think will happen next. Discuss what students have written before returning to the film. As a variation, stop the video at a strategic point, and ask students to respond to the film's content so far.

Assessment Strategies and Rubrics

The information in this section covers a number of areas related to assessing students' writing, including using assessment as a teaching tool, using peer assessment, and using writing portfolios.

An Overview—
Assessment and Instruction

> "Unless we show children how to read their writing, their work will not improve."
>
> —**DONALD GRAVES**

In the past, writing assessment basically fell to the teacher. Students turned in work—then waited to see what grades they would receive. Now it is widely recognized that learning to be a good assessor is one of the best ways to become a strong writer. In order to assess well, students must learn to recognize good writing. They can begin to recognize writing that works, and writing that does not work, by . . .

1. learning about the traits of writing that are used to assess their own and others' work,
2. applying the traits to a wide variety of written texts, and
3. applying the traits to their own work—first assessing it for strengths and weaknesses and then revising it as needed.

Why should students be assessors?

Students who learn to be assessors also learn to . . .

■ think like writers,
■ take more responsibility for their own revising, and
■ make meaningful changes in their writing—instead of simply recopying a draft to make it look neater.

Role of Teachers and Students

Here is a quick summary of the kinds of activities teachers and students usually engage in while acting as assessors in the classroom.

Teachers

As assessors, teachers who match their assessment to instruction engage in . . .

■ roaming the classroom, observing students' work, and offering comments or questions that will help take students to next steps.
■ one-on-one conferences in which students come with a question they need answered.
■ reading student work, using a general *assessment rubric* such as the ones in this guide (pages 176-180).
■ tracking scores over time to calculate a final grade for a grading period.

Students

As assessors, students often engage in . . .

■ reviewing scoring guides, such as the checklist on page 45 in the handbook or the rubrics in this guide.
■ using a *peer response sheet,* such as the one on page 49 in the handbook.
■ assessing and discussing written work that the teacher shares with the class.
■ assessing their own work, using a checklist or rubric.
■ compiling a portfolio and reflecting on the written work included.

Effective Assessment in the Classroom

> "Good assessment starts with a vision of success."
>
> **—RICK STIGGINS**

Good assessment helps students see how they are growing as writers. It indicates to teachers where students are succeeding and where they need help. To ensure that assessment is working in your classroom, you should do the following things:

- Make sure all students know the criteria you will use to assess their writing. If you are going to use a rubric, provide them with copies before they begin writing.

- Send home copies of rubrics or checklists to parents, too, so they can help their children know what is expected of them.

- Make sure your instruction and assessment match. You cannot teach one thing and assess students on another—if you expect them to be successful.

- Involve students regularly in assessing . . .
  - ✔ published work from a variety of sources,
  - ✔ your work (share your writing—even if it's in unfinished draft form), and
  - ✔ their own work.

- Don't grade *everything* students write. Instead, you should encourage students to write *often*; then choose a few pieces to grade.

- Respond to the content *first*. Then look at the conventions. Correctness is important, but if you comment on spelling and mechanics before content, the message to the student is, "I don't care as much about what you say as I do about whether you spell everything correctly."

- Encourage students to save rough drafts and to collect pieces of work regularly in a portfolio. This type of collection helps students see how they are progressing as writers.

Conducting Conferences

Conduct conferences with students at all points during the development of a piece of writing. Here are three common practices that you can use to communicate with student writers during a writing project:

- **Desk-Side Conferences** occur when you stop at a student's desk to ask questions and make responses. Ask open-ended questions to give the writer "space" to talk and clarify his or her own thinking about the writing.

- **Scheduled Conferences** give you and a student a chance to meet in a more structured setting to discuss a specific problem or simply assess his or her progress on a particular piece of writing.

Note: A typical conference should last from 3 to 5 minutes. Always try to praise one thing, ask an appropriate question, and offer one suggestion.

- **Small-Group Conferences** give several students who are at the same stage in the writing process, or who are experiencing similar problems, a chance to meet with you.

The Traits of Good Writing

> "Students are more engaged when indicators of success are clearly spelled out."
>
> **—JUDITH ZORFASS & HARRIET COPEL**

Most students could list the traits of a good friend (loyal, kind, good listener) or the traits of a good taco (meat, lettuce, lots of cheese), but could they list the qualities that make up good writing? As a teacher, it's your job to help students first identify these qualities, or traits, and then learn how to use and talk about them in their own writing.

How the "Traits" Connect to Assessment

Traits are qualities or characteristics that define strong performance in writing. These traits can be summarized in checklists, rubrics, or scoring guides that define performance along a continuum.

Learning to be a good assessor is one of the best ways for students to become strong writers. Students must know and be able to describe the traits that exemplify writing that works, and writing that does not work. Students learn to assess, generally, by following three key steps:

1. learning about the traits of writing that will be used to assess their work,

2. applying the traits to a wide variety of written texts, and

3. applying the traits to their own work—first assessing it for strengths and weaknesses and then revising it as needed.

What writing traits are important?

When teachers across the country are asked to identify and define what they value in good writing, the traits listed below are most often mentioned.

Interesting Ideas

Good writing includes a clear, focused, well-defined subject or thesis and all the details needed to bring the topic to life.

Clear Organization

Good writing contains a strong lead or an order of ideas that makes sense, transitions that link ideas together, and a powerful wrap-up, or conclusion.

Personal Voice

The best writing contains the personal imprint of the writer, clear enthusiasm for the subject, and concern for the informational needs and interests of the audience.

Well-Chosen Words

Good writing shows the writer's skill in finding just the right word or phrase to make meaning clear.

Smooth Sentences

Good writing flows smoothly from one sentence to the next. Sentences are strong, well crafted, and varied.

Correct Copy

Good writing reflects attention to conventions such as spelling, punctuation, grammar, and capitalization.

Note: For more on these traits, see pages 18-21 in *Write on Track*. For a "Traits of Good Writing" rubric for general assessment, see page 180 in this guide.

Assessment Rubrics

This section includes rubrics to assess the following modes of writing: *narrative, descriptive, expository,* and *persuasive.* Use them as indicated here:

Narrative Writing ● Use this rubric with story writing and forms of autobiographical and biographical writing that recall specific events. (See page 176.)

Descriptive Writing ● Use this rubric with descriptive paragraphs and essays. (See page 177.)

Expository Writing ● Use this rubric with informational writing, including how-to writing, expository paragraphs, summaries, feature articles, business letters, etc. (See page 178.)

Persuasive Writing ● Use this rubric with persuasive paragraphs and essays, with letters to the editor, etc. (See page 179.)

Note: There's a "Traits of Good Writing" rubric for general assessment on page 180.

What is a rubric?

A rubric is a list of criteria by which a piece of writing is assessed. It should include a list of traits or qualities that demonstrate what makes a piece of writing effective. Students should always know beforehand what criteria will be used to assess their writing.

How do I use the rubrics to score writing?

The rubrics list the traits of effective writing as explained in the handbook (the same traits used to assess writing on many state writing-assessment tests).

Each rubric is based on a 5-point rating scale. A score of 5 means that the writing strongly addresses a particular trait. A score of 3 means the writing is average or still developing that trait. Finally, a score of 1 means that the writing is still in the beginning stages, showing little development of that trait. (*Note:* A piece of writing need not exhibit all of the descriptors under each trait to be effective.)

The rubrics may be used to assess works in progress as well as final drafts, and may be modified to meet the needs of the students or the writing being assessed.

Do not combine and average the scores on the rubric to come up with an overall score for the student. Seeing separate scores for the traits allows students to see where they need to improve and where their strengths lie. It is also important to give students an opportunity to assess their work and make changes *before* it is marked with a final score or grade.

After students have completed their revisions, and it is time for you to assess their final efforts, remember to respond to content first and then conventions. You may want to make some comments about each paper as a whole, either on sticky notes or at the end of the work.

How can I use the rubrics as a teaching tool?

Work with students in a whole-class activity to evaluate a piece of writing, using a rubric as a guide. At first, you may focus on one specific trait (like *ideas* or *organization*).

Later on, students can evaluate a selection for several traits. The more they practice evaluation, the more comfortable they will become with this "writer's language" and begin to exhibit the traits in their own writing.

ASSESSMENT RUBRIC

Narrative Writing: Personal Narrative

A personal narrative is a story about a personal memory. A personal narrative is sometimes called a memoir or an all-about-me story.

____ **IDEAS**
- The writing shares interesting details of a personal experience.
- The writing is clear, focused, and well developed.

____ **ORGANIZATION**
- The writing has a beginning, a middle, and an ending.
- The sequence of events tells a clear story.

____ **VOICE**
- The writing is personal and unique.
- The writing reveals the writer's feelings about the experience.

____ **WORD CHOICE**
- The writing includes lively verbs and original expressions.
- The writing uses specific nouns and colorful adjectives.

____ **SMOOTH SENTENCES**
- The sentences are smooth and easy to read.
- The sentences have a variety of beginnings and lengths.
- Dialogue, when used, adds life to the story.

____ **CORRECT COPY**
- The writing uses capital letters for sentence beginnings and names.
- Conventional spelling, punctuation, and grammar are used.

Scoring Guide

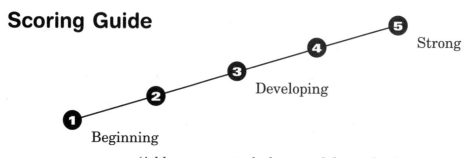

1 Beginning
2
3 Developing
4
5 Strong

(Add comments to the bottom of the student's paper.)

ASSESSMENT RUBRIC

Descriptive Writing: Descriptive Paragraph

Descriptive writing *shows* readers a subject rather than simply *telling* them about it. This is done by using details discovered through the senses (sight, sound, smell, feeling) and other colorful language.

____ IDEAS
- The writing focuses on one subject.
- The writing uses details about the senses.

____ ORGANIZATION
- The writing gives readers a clear picture of the subject.
- The writing has a beginning, a middle, and an ending.

____ VOICE
- The writing shows the writer's interest in the subject.

____ WORD CHOICE
- Specific nouns and vivid verbs help readers picture the subject.
- Colorful describing words add life to the writing.

____ SMOOTH SENTENCES
- The writing has a variety of sentence beginnings and lengths.
- The writing is easy to follow.

____ CORRECT COPY
- The writing uses capital letters for sentence beginnings and proper nouns.
- The writing uses correct grammar, spelling, and punctuation.

Scoring Guide

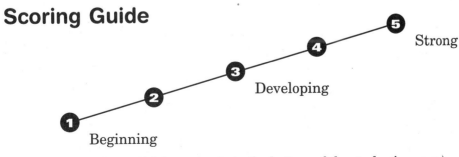

(Add comments to the bottom of the student's paper.)

ASSESSMENT RUBRIC

Expository Writing: How-To Writing

Directions tell the readers how to do things. Sometimes directions are written in list form, and other times they are written in paragraphs. The steps are often numbered.

____ **IDEAS**
- The writing explains a specific way to do or make something.
- The directions are clear and easy to follow.

____ **ORGANIZATION**
- The writing has a beginning, a middle, and an ending.
- The writing contains appropriate transition words or numbers.

____ **VOICE**
- The writing is engaging and speaks clearly to the reader.

____ **WORD CHOICE**
- The writing contains specific terms and definitions, when needed.

____ **SMOOTH SENTENCES**
- The sentences are smooth and easy to read.
- The sentences present a variety of beginnings and lengths.

____ **CORRECT COPY**
- The writing uses capital letters for sentence beginnings and proper nouns.
- Conventional spelling, punctuation, and grammar are used.

Scoring Guide

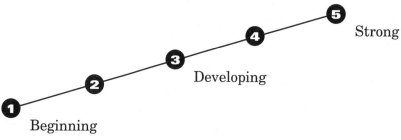

(Add comments to the bottom of the student's paper.)

ASSESSMENT RUBRIC

Persuasive Writing: Persuasive Paragraph

In persuasive writing, the writer shares an opinion about a current issue or concern. Writers usually present the situation and then tell what they would like to see happen.

____ **IDEAS**
- The writing states the importance of the issue.
- The writing shares the writer's feelings and calls for a certain action.

____ **ORGANIZATION**
- Necessary background information is explained.
- Important details are included.

____ **VOICE**
- The writing shows the writer's genuine concern for this cause.

____ **WORD CHOICE**
- The writing uses words to create strong feelings in the reader.

____ **SMOOTH SENTENCES**
- The sentences move smoothly from start to finish.
- The sentences present a variety of beginnings and lengths.

____ **CORRECT COPY**
- The writing uses punctuation marks and capital letters correctly.
- All facts have been checked, and names are spelled correctly.

Scoring Guide

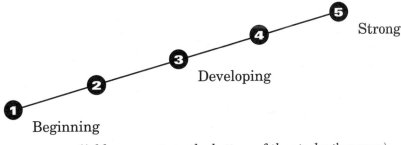

(Add comments to the bottom of the student's paper.)

ASSESSMENT RUBRIC

Traits of Good Writing

____ **IDEAS**
- The writing has an easy-to-identify main message.
- The writing makes sense.
- The writing includes specific, interesting details about the topic.

____ **ORGANIZATION**
- The writing has a beginning that sets up what follows.
- The middle expands upon the main idea.
- The ending brings the writing to a close.

____ **VOICE**
- The writing shows enthusiasm, expressiveness, and individuality.
- The writing is fun to share aloud.

____ **WORD CHOICE**
- Specific, interesting words make the writing clear and enjoyable to read.
- The words seem just right for the topic and audience.

____ **SMOOTH SENTENCES**
- The sentences are smooth and easy to read.
- The sentences have a variety of beginnings and lengths.

____ **CORRECT COPY**
- Conventional spelling, punctuation, capitalization, and grammar are used.
- The paper is formatted properly.

Scoring Guide

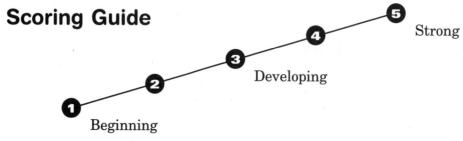

(Add comments to the bottom of the student's paper.)

What About Basic Skills?

Research indicates that the study of grammar apart from a writing context has no real impact on writing quality (except for the implementation of the types of activities listed on this page).

Of course, students need some basic understanding of grammar and mechanics to produce accurate final drafts of papers.

Student writers can find the help they need in a handy guide to the rules of grammar and usage (such as the "Proofreader's Guide" in the *Write on Track* handbook).

How can I promote meaningful grammar instruction?

The following types of activities will help students gain a better understanding of grammar and mechanics:

- Link grammar work as much as possible to the students' own writing.
- Simply note a problem. Don't make a big issue of it. Make it clear to the student what the problem is and why it is a problem.
- Then direct the student to the pages in the handbook so he or she can see how to correct the problem.
- Also have the student keep track of this error in a special section of a notebook or a writing folder, so he or she will know what to look for the next time a piece of writing must be edited and proofread.
- If one problem demands special attention, or is common to many students in the class, teach a direct lesson on the skill, or a related minilesson or activity sheet. (See pages 206-244 in this guide for minilessons.)
- Remind students that you expect them to watch for certain problems in future writing.
- Assess those conventions you have taught.

- Immerse students in all aspects of language learning: reading, writing, speaking, listening, and thinking. Educator James Moffett says the standard dialect is "most effectively mastered through imitating speech."
- Ask students to correct only pieces that go through the entire writing process; it's not necessary to correct or assess all writing assignments or journal entries.
- Don't overwhelm students with too much grammar. Find out which skills give your students problems and focus your instruction accordingly.
- You may want to keep a poster-sized list of frequently misspelled words displayed in the classroom. Encourage students to be responsible for spelling these words correctly.

What approaches can I use?

Sentence combining: Use the students' own writing as much as possible. Stress the reason for combining ideas and the proper punctuation for combining.

Sentence revising: Give students practice adding and changing information in sentences that they have already created. Let them work together to revise one another's writing.

Sentence transforming: Have students change sentences from one form to another (from passive to active, beginning a sentence in a different way, and so on).

Using Writing Portfolios

Many teachers are making portfolios an important part of their writing programs. Will portfolios work for you? Will they help you and your students assess their writing? Read on and find out.

What is a writing portfolio?

A writing portfolio is a collection of a student's writing for evaluation. A portfolio is different from the traditional writing folder. A writing folder (also known as a working folder) contains *all* of a student's work; a portfolio contains only selected pieces.

There are two basic types of portfolios. A *showcase portfolio* is usually presented for evaluation at the end of a grading period. As the name implies, it should contain a selection of a student's best work. A *growth portfolio* notes the way in which a writer is changing and growing. This type of portfolio is usually collected regularly—say, once a month—throughout the year. (See pages 28-31 in the handbook for more information.)

Why should students compile portfolios?

Having students compile writing portfolios makes the whole process of writing more meaningful to them. They will more willingly put forth their best efforts as they work on various writing projects, knowing that they are accountable for producing a certain number of finished pieces. They may more easily see writing as a process of drafting, sharing, and rewriting, knowing that this process leads to better writing. And they may be more willing to carefully polish finished pieces (for showcase portfolios).

How many pieces of writing should be included in a portfolio?

Although you and your students will best be able to decide this, we advise that students compile at least two to three pieces of writing in a showcase portfolio each quarter. (The number of pieces in a growth portfolio may vary from month to month.) All of the drafts should be included for each piece. Students should also be expected to include a reflective writing that assesses their own writing progress at the end of each quarter or semester. (See page 183.)

When do portfolios work best?

Portfolios work best when students have sufficient class time to work on their writing in order to produce effective portfolios. If they are used correctly, portfolios help turn beginning writers into practicing writers who are able to use regularly scheduled blocks of time to "practice" their craft, to think, talk, and explore options in their writing.

How can I help my students with their portfolio writing?

Have students explore topics of real interest to them. Also allow them to write for different purposes and audiences and in many different forms. Schedule sharing sessions.

In addition, encourage students to try evaluating their own writing and the writing of their peers as it develops. Have them use the rubrics on pages 176-180. Pages 183-184 include the following blackline masters:

- Writing Reflections
- Tracking Your Writing

How do I grade a portfolio?

Base each grade or assessment on goals you and your students establish beforehand and on what is achieved in the portfolio. Many teachers develop a critique sheet for assessment based on the goals established by the class. An overall assessment honors the students' efforts. Consider (1) quality of content, (2) effective presentation, and (3) thoughtful self-reflection.

Name _____   Date _____

Writing Reflections

I decided to put this piece of writing in my portfolio because

_____

_____

_____

_____

As I worked on this piece, I learned _____

_____

_____

_____

_____

In my future writing, I would like to _____

_____

_____

_____

Name _____

Tracking Your Writing

Date _____

Title _____

1. **Read your draft to yourself.** ☐

2. **Read your draft two times to a partner.** ☐

3. **My partner's questions and suggestions:** ☐

_____

_____

_____

4. **Revise your draft.** (For example, add information if you need to.) ☐

5. **Edit your draft for complete sentences.** ☐

    Edit your draft for the best and right words. ☐

6. **Proofread your draft for spelling.** ☐

    Proofread for punctuation and capital letters. ☐

7. **Teacher conference** _____ ☐
                                   (Date)

8. **Final teacher check** _____ ☐
                                   (Date)

Reading Strategies

The strategies on the following pages will help you promote personalized, active reading in your classroom.

Responding to Literature

When students respond to something they have read, they are creating meaning. The responses can be written, oral, or hands-on projects. The responses can be intellectual, full of feeling, or a combination of both. Whatever the response, moving beyond the literal, factual details is important for comprehension.

Written Responses

Poems and Songs

- Write an alphabet poem about one of the characters in the book. The first line could be the character's name.
- Write a jingle about the book. Use the tune of "Row, Row, Row Your Boat" or "Twinkle, Twinkle, Little Star" for the jingle.
- Make up some couplets (two lines that rhyme) about the characters or information in the book. If you like, retell the whole story in a series of couplets.

Notes and Letters

- Write a letter to the author of the book. Tell the author what you liked best about the book. If there was something about the book that you didn't like, or a question you had, tell the author about that, too. Finally, give the author one last special thought about the book.
- Write a note to one of the characters in the book. Tell the character about something you may have in common with each other.

Other Written Responses

- Write a script (like lines in a play) for one of your favorite scenes from the book. Use the script in a reader's theater performance or a puppet show.

- Write a news story about an event in the book. Remember to answer the 5 W's and come up with a catchy headline.

Oral Responses

Creative Dramatics

- Place an empty chair in front of a group and then proceed to introduce a character from the book—as if the character is sitting right there on the chair.

Games

- Play "twenty questions" with other students who have read the same book. Any member of the group can ask questions, and anyone can answer the questions.

Short Talks

- Create a commercial to sell the book; use props if you can make them or they are available. Present this live or record it on video.
- Create a multimedia presentation based on the book.

Drawing and Painting

- Draw or paint a portrait of one of the characters from the book. Make a decorative frame that somehow relates to the theme of the book.

Other Projects

- Make a crossword puzzle or word search of new or interesting words you found as you were reading. Share the puzzle or word search with others who have read the same book.

Reading-Writing Lists

THE PROCESS OF WRITING

Arthur Writes a Story
Marc Brown

Author: A True Story
Helen Lester

Speaking of Journals: Children's Writers Talk about Their Diaries, Notebooks and Sketchbooks
Paula W. Graham

What Do Authors Do?
Eileen Christelow

WRITING IN JOURNALS

Amelia Writes Again!
Marissa Moss

Castle Diary: The Journal of Tobias Burgess, Page
Richard Platt

Celia's Island Journal
Celia Thaxter (adapted by Loretta Krupinski)

Diary of a Drummer Boy
Marlene Targ Brill

Dilly's Big Sister Diary
Cynthia Copeland Lewis

Dilly's Summer Camp Diary
Cynthia Copeland Lewis

Emma's Journal: The Story of a Colonial Girl
Marissa Moss

Good-Bye for Today
Peter and Connie Roop

Hannah's Journal: The Story of an Immigrant Girl
Marissa Moss

It's a Frog's Life
Steve Parker

Look to the Earth: A Wolf Pup Diary
Jean Craighead George

Rachel's Journal: The Story of a Pioneer Girl
Marissa Moss

Running Girl: The Diary of Ebonee Rose
Sharon Bell Mathis

The Top-Secret Journal of Fiona Claire Jardin
Robin Cruise

PERSONAL NARRATIVES

Amelia and Eleanor Go for a Ride
Pam Munoz Ryan

Boy of the Deeps
Ian Wallace

Jingle Dancer
Cynthia L. Smith

Journey Home
Lawrence McKay, Jr.

July
James Stevenson

Looking Back: A Book of Memories
Lois Lowry

Molly Bannaky
Alice McGill

The Rag Coat
Lauren Mills

Seeing the Circle
Joseph Bruchac

Smoky Nights
Eve Bunting

Tallchief: America's Prima Ballerina
Maria Tallchief

Tell Me a Tale: A Book About Storytelling
Joseph Bruchac

Through My Eyes
Ruby Bridges

Thunder Cake
Patricia Polacco

26 Fairmount Avenue
Tomie dePaola

Vacation in the Village: A Story from West Africa
Pierre Yves Njeng

The Wall
Eve Bunting

When I Lived with Bats
Faith McNulty

Wild Horses I Have Known
Hope Ryden

MAKING ALBUMS

Anastasia's Album
Hugh Brewster

Brown Angels: An Album of Pictures and Verse
Walter Dean Myers

Carl Makes a Scrapbook
Alexandra Day

Circus: An Album
Linda Granfield

Cowboy: An Album
Linda Granfield

My Book About My Cat
Sheldon Gertensfeld, V.M.D.

My Book About My Dog
Sheldon Gertensfeld, V.M.D.

My Fellow Americans: A Family Album
Alice Provensen

LISTS

The Book of Lists for Kids
Sandra Choron

Can You Spot the Spotted Dog?
John Rowe

Dark Day, Light Night
Jan Carr

Fantastic Book of 1001 Lists
Russell Ash

Glasses: Who Needs 'Em?
Lane Smith

Moon Glows
Berthea verDorn

Summer Reading Is Killing Me
Jon Scieszka

FRIENDLY NOTES

How to Make Pop-Ups
Joan Irvine

Postcards from Pluto: A Tour of the Solar System
Loreen Leedy

Stringbean's Trip to the Shining Sea
Vera B. Williams

Toot and Puddle
Holly Hobbie

FRIENDLY LETTERS

Dear Annie
Judith Caseley

Kate Heads West
Pat Brisson

The Kid's Address Book: Over 2,000 Addresses of Celebrities, Athletes, Entertainers, and More—Just for Kids
Michael Levine

Letters from Felix
Annette Langen and Constanza Droop

Mouse Letters
Michelle Cartlidge

My Dear Noel: The Story of a Letter from Beatrix Potter
Jane Johnson

Your Best Friend, Kate
Pat Brisson

FAMILY STORIES

A Band of Angels: A Story Inspired by the Jubilee Singers
Deborah Hopkinson

A Birthday Basket for Tia
Pat Mora

The Canada Geese Quilt
Natalie Kinsey-Warnock

A Forever Family
Roslyn Banish

Go Fish
Mary Stolz

Laura's Album: A Remembrance Scrapbook of Laura Ingalls Wilder
William Anderson

The Lost Lake
Allen Say

Maria's Comet
Deborah Hopkinson

The Moon Lady
Amy Tan

"More, More, More," Said the Baby: Three Love Stories
Vera B. Williams

My Great-Aunt Arizona
Gloria Houston

Serefina Under the Circumstances
Phyllis Theroux

Tea with Milk
Allen Say

Through the Eyes of Your Ancestors: A Step-by-Step Guide to Uncovering Your Family's History
Maureen Taylor

True Heart
Marissa Moss

The Wednesday Surprise
Eve Bunting

ALPHABET BOOKS

A Is for Amos
Deborah Chandra

A to Z, Do You Ever Feel Like Me?
Bonnie Hausman

Aardvarks, Disembark!
Ann Jonas

Alison's Zinnia
Anita Lobel

Alpha Beta Chowder
Jeanne Steig

Alphabestiary
Jane Yolen

Away from Home
Anita Lobel

City Seen from A to Z
Rachel Isadora

The Disappearing Alphabet
Richard Wilbur

Everything to Spend the Night—From A to Z
Ann Whitford Paul

Jeremy Kooloo
Tim Mahurin

K Is for Kwanzaa: A Kwanzaa Alphabet Book
Juwanda Ford

Let's Fly from A to Z
Doug Magee and Robert Newman

Many Nations: An Alphabet of Native America
Joseph Bruchac

Once Upon A to Z: An Alphabet Odyssey
Jody Linscott

Pedro, His Perro, and the Alphabet Sombrero
Lynn Rowe

The Sailor's Alphabet
Michael McCurdy

Sharon, Lois & Bram Sing A to Z
Sharon Hampson et al.

Spring: An Alphabet Acrostic
Steven Schnur

NEWSPAPER STORIES

Extra! Extra!: The Who, What, Where, When and Why of Newspapers
Linda Granfield

The Furry News: How to Make a Newspaper
Loreen Leedy

Johnny on the Sport
Edward Sorel

The Young Journalist's Book: How to Write and Produce Your Own Newspaper
Donna Guthrie

HOW-TO WRITING

Air and Flight
Jon Richards

All Around Town: The Photographs of Richard Samuel Roberts
Dinah Johnson

Angela Weaves a Dream: The Story of a Young Maya Artist
Michael Sola

Art with Carmen Lomas Garza
Carmen Lomas Garza

Creepy Cuisine
Lucy Monroe

The Elements of Pop-Up: A Pop-Up Book for Aspiring Paper Engineers
David A. Carter

Everybody Cooks Rice
Norah Dooley

From Pictures to Words: A Book About Making a Book
Janet Stevens

Green Fun: Plants as Play
Marianne Haug Gjersvik

Grow It Again
Elizabeth Macleod

Hopscotch Around the World
Mary Lankford

LaCrosse: The National Game of the Iroquois
Diane Hoyt-Goldsmith

Making Magic Windows: Creating Papel Picado/Cut-Paper Art
Carmen Lomas Garza

My Indoor Garden
Carol Lerner

Sewing by Hand
Christine Hoffman

Snowflake Bentley
Jacqueline Briggs Martin

Water and Boats
Jon Richards

REALISTIC STORIES

Abigail Takes the Wheel
Avi

Amber Brown Is Not a Crayon
Paula Danziger

The Babe and I
David Adler

Brooklyn, Bugsy, and Me
Lynea Bowdish

Buster Makes the Grade
Marc Brown and Stephen Krensky

Girls Together
Sherley Ann Williams

Gowanus Dogs
Jonathan Frost

Howie Bowles, Secret Agent
Kate Banks

I Have an Olive Tree
Eve Bunting

I'm José and I'm Okay: Three Stories from Bolivia
Werner Holzwarth

Jumping into Nothing
Gina Willner-Pardo

Just Juice
Karen Hesse

La Mariposa
Francisco Jimenez

Last Licks: A Spaldeen Story
Cari Best

Marianthe's Story: Painted Words, Spoken Memories
Aliki

Mimmy & Sophie
Miriam Cohen

Mr. Stumpguss Is a Third Grader
Kathleen Duey

Not My Dog
Colby Rodowsky

Pony Trouble
Dale Blackwell Gasque

Rosy Cole Discovers America
Sheila Greenwald

Roz and Ozzie
Johanna Hurwitz

Sable
Karen Hesse

Strong to the Hoop
John Coy

Thank You, Mr. Falker
Patricia Polacco

The Ugly Vegetables
Grace Lin

Voices in the Park
Anthony Browne

When Agnes Caws
Candace Fleming

When This World Was New
D. H. Figueredo

TIME-TRAVEL FANTASIES

Alien for Rent
Betsy Duffey

The Door in the Lake
Nancy Butts

A Flying Birthday Cake?
Louis Sachar

My Trip to Alpha I
A. Slote

The Nose from Jupiter
Richard Scrimger

Sector 7
David Wiesner

Sleeping Boy
Sonia Craddock

This Mess
Pam Conrad

Time Train
Paul Fleischman

Weslandia
Paul Fleischman

Wilbur's Space Machine
Lorna Balian

FREE-VERSE POETRY

And the Green Grass Grew All Around
Collected by Alvin Schwartz

Creatures of Earth, Sea, and Sky
Georgia Heard

Doodle Dandies: Poems That Take Shape
J. Patrick Lewis

Flicker Flash
Joan Bransfield Graham

Follow the Moon
Sarah Weeks

Hand in Hand: An American History Through Poetry
Edited by Lee Bennett Hopkins

Night on Neighborhood Street
Eloise Greenfield

Sing to the Sun
Ashley Bryan

Wake Up House!: Rooms Full of Poems
Dee Lillegard

Who Bop?
Jonathan London

Reading-at-Home Contract

During this quarter, I will read _____ minutes _____ times a week.

I may choose the books I want to read. I should read books that I can understand, but I should not read books that are too easy. Sometimes I can read a difficult book with a partner.

☐ I will keep a list of the books or stories that I read.

☐ Each week I will report to my teacher about my success with this contract.

☐ I will try to write down how long I read each time. Someone may help me keep track.

_____   _____
(Student signature)   (Teacher signature)

_____   _____
(Date)   (Date)

_____
(Parent signature)

_____
(Date)

Books I Am Reading

BOOK TITLE	Author	Time (minutes)

Thinking and Learning Strategies

The thinking and learning strategies on the following pages cover important areas often included in a complete language program.

Writing to Learn

What is "writing to learn"?

Writing to learn is a method of learning that students can use in all subjects at all ages. It is thinking on paper—thinking to discover connections, describe processes, express newly discovered ideas, raise questions, and find answers.

How can I get started with writing to learn?

Before introducing writing-to-learn activities into your curriculum, remember these key points:

- The main purpose of writing-to-learn activities is to promote better thinking and learning; better writing is a by-product.

- Since writing-to-learn activities allow students to personalize learning, they understand better and remember longer.

- Writing to learn is not a "program." Writing-to-learn activities complement the curriculum already being used in different subject areas.

How do I implement writing to learn?

- With your students, turn to pages 274-275 in *Write on Track* to develop an understanding of writing to learn.

- Select writing-to-learn activities that suit your subject area and allow your students to become more independent and more actively involved in the learning process.

- Help students understand that they are "writing to learn" and not "writing to show learning." With writing-to-learn activities, they are not writing to please you, the teacher, but to better understand information.

What other strategies can I use to incorporate writing-to-learn activities?

- Use any of the writing-to-learn activities listed on pages 274-275 in the handbook.
- Use journal writing regularly in your classroom to develop students' responding and thinking skills.

Class Journal ● You may have students use a notebook journal to respond to class-related work and events. For example, after you introduce a new concept in science, have students predict what might happen next. Or ask students to respond to a class discussion or a video. Class journals work especially well for responding to reading. Class discussions become more engaging when students have first responded in their journals and then are able to share those responses orally. Class journals can help students raise questions, develop answers, and respond to any class activity.

Project Journal ● This journal is like the class journal except that it is a more independent writing-to-learn tool. Students use this journal to keep track of their progress on a project over a period of days or weeks. Project journals, like class journals, allow students to jot down new vocabulary related to the class or project, record important or confusing ideas, make predictions about what might happen, and connect concepts to personal experiences and ideas.

Personal Journal ● This notebook allows the student to respond independently. Responses and reflections are not assigned. The student uses this notebook (sometimes called a learning log) to question and describe concepts discovered in various classes. Such writing allows students to develop abstract thinking skills. They may choose to use this journal as a communication tool to dialogue with the teacher about questions or concerns.

Collaborative Learning

We have all participated in collaborative groups at some point in our lives—in our families, with friends, in sports activities. Cooperation is an essential skill for getting along successfully in society. Collaborative learning means "working together." It differs from group work in that collaborative learning stresses positive interdependence among students, face-to-face interaction, individual accountability, interpersonal and small-group skills, and group processing. These basic elements can lead students to high achievement, positive attitudes toward subject areas, and stronger critical-thinking skills.

How can I get started with collaborative learning?

As you begin implementing collaborative groups in your classroom, remember these key points:

- Collaborative learning can be used successfully with any type of learning activity, but it works best with activities that involve problem solving, decision making, or creative thinking.
- Collaborative groups should be small (2-6 students) and include students of varied abilities.
- Students must learn and practice collaborative skills before cooperative learning can be successful.
- With collaborative learning, the teacher structures learning groups, teaches basic concepts and strategies, monitors groups, and assists as needed.

How do I implement collaborative learning?

There are a number of issues to consider:

- Begin by teaching students collaborative skills. Review pages 236-237 and 280-283 of *Write on Track* for ideas about developing listening skills and group skills.

- Arrange the room (desks or tables in small groupings) to best implement collaborative learning.
- Design learning tasks that will be best accomplished through collaborative learning. (Don't assign a task to a group that can best be completed individually.)
- Introduce concepts and strategies to the whole class.
- Divide students into assigned groups and provide them with roles (such as leader, reporter) to fill within the group.
- Monitor group functioning and assist when clarification of tasks or roles is necessary.
- After the task is completed, review the process. Discuss successes and areas that require better group functioning.

Making Classroom Presentations

Recommended Group and Size:
A heterogeneous group of four students

Group Skills to Emphasize:
"Learning to Listen" (pages 236-237)
"Thinking Clearly" (pages 268-273)
"Working in Groups" (pages 280-283)

Other Skills to Emphasize:
"Giving Short Talks" (pages 244-251)
"Performance Tips" (page 242)

The Process:
Step 1: Students work together in their groups to prepare a presentation on an assigned topic. They decide on each group member's role. Students create visual aids and rehearse presentations.
Step 2: Each group presents to the whole class.

Assessment:
Each student in the group takes an active part in an informative, well-planned presentation.

Learning to Think

Of course your students are already thinking! Encouraging clear, creative thinking is the goal of any effective learning environment.

Promoting Thinking Skills

Here are some ways to make your classroom more "thinking oriented."

- Creative learning activities and environments enhance thinking skills.
- Students' thinking skills improve through modeling, practice, and experimentation.

Implementing Thinking Skills

- Personalize the learning because students approach learning more thoughtfully when the subject matter means something to them personally.
- Promote creative activities that enhance thinking skills: writing stories, poems, riddles, songs; doing problem solving.
- Use collaborative learning, which encourages verbalization, a powerful way to learn and think.
- Challenge students to think and act by asking open-ended questions and by initiating role-playing activities and discussions.
- Discuss different kinds of thinking and ways to think clearly. (See *Write on Track,* pages 268-273, for help.)
- Help students think about their own learning and connect what they have already learned to new information.

Consider Multiple Intelligences

It is widely accepted that people learn best in different ways. When planning class projects, consider the following natural abilities:

- to compose and understand music (musical)
- to perform balanced, controlled body movements (kinesthetic)
- to make complex logical or mathematical calculations (mathematical)
- to learn and use language (linguistic)
- to visualize things not seen (spatial)
- to interact with others and understand behaviors (interpersonal)
- to understand and sense the "self" (intrapersonal)
- to identify and understand patterns in nature (naturalist)

Thinking in Action

Return to the handbook throughout the school year as situations in class work and school life call for the following thinking strategies.

Problem-Solving Strategies

- After a lesson that presents a problem, have students in small groups follow the steps listed on page 269 in *Write on Track* to discover possible solutions.
- Read aloud from a story in which the main character faces a problem. Stop reading before the problem is resolved and ask students to write in their journals about how they would have the character solve the problem.

Decision-Making Strategies

- Have students participate in decisions that affect your classroom. Present two or three options; then arrange students in small groups to work through the decision—using the guidelines listed on page 270 in *Write on Track*.

Clear-Thinking Strategies

- Read the class a short essay containing both factual statements and opinion statements. Discuss which statements are factual and which are opinions. (*Write on Track* page 271 will help.)
- Study some TV, magazine, and newspaper advertisements with your students. Separate the facts and the opinions presented. (See *Write on Track,* page 234, about viewing commercials.)

Building Vocabulary

We know there is a strong connection between a student's vocabulary and his or her listening, speaking, and writing ability. The stronger a student's vocabulary, the more effectively he or she is able to communicate. The following section provides insights and strategies for helping students build their vocabulary skills.

How can I get started?

Before you implement strategies for improving vocabulary, remember these key points:

- Vocabulary development must occur within the context of specific subject areas. Students must read, hear, speak, and write the words they are attempting to learn in each of their classes.
- Giving students lists of vocabulary words with little or no context is not an efficient way to teach vocabulary.
- Students learn words by connecting them to their own experiences.

How can students begin building their vocabulary skills?

- Examine and discuss with your students the vocabulary section in *Write on Track* (pages 209-215).
- Involve students in creating vocabulary lists. Choose from relevant themes, topics, subjects, and events in the classroom.
- Encourage students to collect personal vocabulary words in their journals. Help them analyze personal and classroom vocabulary words using a dictionary, glossary, or thesaurus.
- Teach students how to use nearby words (context) to determine meanings of new vocabulary words. (*Write on Track* page 210 can help.)
- Design writing activities that encourage students to use newly acquired vocabulary words in context.

Strategies for Building Vocabulary Skills

In addition to the strategies provided in *Write on Track* (pages 209-215), try the following vocabulary-building activities:

- Select five or six words from a chapter or selection students are about to read. Direct them to the locations of the words in the text, and ask them to write down what they think each word means. Discuss possible meanings and arrive at correct definitions from context.
- Select a word from one of your class vocabulary lists. Show students how to use a thesaurus to find the word and its synonyms. Have partners select words from the vocabulary list, look them up in a thesaurus, and share the synonyms with their partners.
- Play a dictionary game, choosing a word from the class list. Without saying the word, tell students the word's definition. Have students race to find the correct word in their dictionaries. The student who finds the correct word first chooses the next definition.
- Encourage students (in small groups or individually) to make up their own word games. These promote creative exploration of new vocabulary words.
- Have students create their own dictionaries of words and definitions that relate to specific themes, especially those being studied in class.
- At the beginning of each day, present a new vocabulary word related to a topic the students are studying. As students enter the room, they immediately grab a dictionary or textbook and look up the word. As a class, students discuss the word, agree on its definition, and use the word correctly in a sentence to show that they know what the word means. A written quiz can be given each Friday, covering the week's five words.

Improving Student Spelling

Students learn to spell over time through experiences with words. Because spelling is a special cognitive process connected to writing and reading, teach it in context—not isolation. Teaching in context helps students see that correct spelling allows writers—themselves included—to communicate ideas clearly. The following section will help you design an effective spelling program.

Getting Started

Before implementing a variety of spelling activities, remember these key points:

- Spelling ability is not an indicator of intelligence. Students who have difficulty with spelling tend to process information holistically, while good spellers tend to process information sequentially.
- Effective spelling programs encourage students to explore relationships between letters and sounds and to discover word patterns. Active word play is a helpful learning tool.
- Spelling improves when students understand why words are spelled the way they are.

Note: Memorizing word lists does not transfer to daily writing.

Guidelines for Teaching Spelling

- Involve students in developing a class spelling list of frequently used words and words from topics explored in class. Study these words in fairly short lists.
- From the class list, help students develop personal spelling lists that fit their abilities, interests, and needs.
- Follow a pretest-study-test pattern. Have students correct their own pretests.
- Focus on sounds and structures of words so that students begin to recognize patterns and develop generalizations.
- Conduct an ongoing analysis of spelling errors so that students learn to self-correct their spelling.

- Teach spelling through the many activities students participate in each day.
- Associate spelling words with students' previous knowledge.
- Write often and build proofreading activities into the writing process.

Strategies for Improving Student Spelling

Consider the following activities and ideas when planning weekly spelling units.

Minilessons: Use the spelling-related minilessons in this guide, or create your own.

Pretest: Select 20-25 words from the master list in the handbook (pages 312-315) to use as a pretest at the beginning of the year. Students who have mastered these words should choose words from their personal lists for weekly spelling practice.

Regular Writing: Encourage students to use words from their weekly spelling lists in journal writing, writing assignments, and other writing activities.

Word Searches: Ask students to look for words from their weekly spelling lists in books, magazines, and newspapers as they read in class and on their own.

Mnemonic Devices: Teach students to create and use mnemonics to remember spelling patterns. Share these devices with the class on student-designed posters.

Theme Dictionaries: Have students list and spell correctly key words related to topics studied in all their classes.

Creative Words: Have students use familiar prefixes and suffixes to create real words that could be added to personal spelling lists and used as weekly spelling practice.

Spelling Starts: Use a short period each day to teach spelling. Then apply that instruction throughout the day's reading and writing activities.

Weekly Spelling Words

1 (long $\bar{i}$ sound spelled *igh*)
bright
climb
fight
gym
high
might
right
sight
tonight

2 (many spelled with *ough*)
bought
enough
fought
idea
island
listen
rough
thought
zipper

3 (many spelled with *ou*)
blood
could
country
cousin
group
lunch
trouble
uncle
would

4 (many spelled with *ou*)
both
ground
loud
mouse
mouth
own
power
round
young

5 (most spelled with *ea*)
bear
break
breakfast
care
dead
instead
ready
wear
weather

6 (spelled with *ea*)
dear
early
earth
heard
heart
learn
leave
really
reason

7 (most spelled with *au*)
answer
aunt
beautiful
because
caught
cause
daughter
laugh
taught

8 (most spelled with *oi* or *ai*)
grade
jail
join
mail
maybe
noise
paint
stairs
voice

9 (most spelled with *ie*)
believe
cheese
dream
either
field
movie
piece
quiet
science

10 (short $\breve{u}$ sound spelled *o*)
another
cover
dirty
front
honey
other
word
world
worry

11 (long $\bar{u}$ sound or end with long $\bar{o}$)
few
follow
hello
huge
loose
poor
sure
usual
window

12 (many spelled with *or* or *ur*)
engine
forget
forgive
giant
hurry
hurt
machine
picture
special

13 (mostly names of months)
April
August
December
February
January
July
people
woman
women

14 (mostly names of months)
June
March
May
November
October
often
once
September
wrong

15 (mostly days of the week)
Friday
Monday
neighbor
Saturday
Sunday
their
Thursday
Tuesday
Wednesday

16 Semester Review

17 (contractions)
aren't
didn't
doesn't
I'll
I'm
isn't
it's
wasn't
you're

18 (end in *-ed*)
asked
decided
dressed
dropped
finished
knocked
pleased
reached
scared

19 (most words plurals)
bushes
clothes
dollars
folks
inches
music
ocean
o'clock
parents

20 (most words compounds)
almost
always
anybody
everyone
everything
nobody
nothing
someone
something

21 (silent letters)
built
dumb
ghost
guess
half
knew
knife
know
whole

22 (consonant blends and digraphs)
catch
desk
kitchen
past
question
report
rest
watch
which

23 (consonant blends and digraphs)
north
pretty
scream
small
spring
strong
surprise
threw
truth

24 (consonant blends and digraphs)
change
dance
flew
floor
flying
kept
orange
strange
understand

25 (consonant blends and digraphs)
angry
bunch
children
crazy
drive
finger
first
forest
hungry

26 (hard to spell)
afraid
again
alone
asleep
captain
favorite
finally
probably
xylophone

27 (hard to spell)
interest
library
minute
planet
police
president
rocket
secret
visit

28 (hard to spell)
animal
different
famous
happiness
hospital
important
metal
middle
pencil

29 (hard to spell)
author
better
mirror
monster
paper
remember
river
together
winter

30 (many are prepositions)
behind
inside
near
outside
person
quick
toward
upon
zebra

31 (many are prepositions)
after
body
during
happen
phone
since
through
until
without

32 Semester Review

Additional Spelling Activities

Teachers can consider the ideas and activities listed on this page when planning weekly spelling lists.

Commonly Mixed Pairs ● We recommend that students make up sentences with commonly mixed pairs of words. These words in the weekly spelling lists have homophones: *would, bear, break, heard, dear, aunt, piece, knew, know, whole, which, threw, metal, poor, it's,* and *you're.* (See pages 316-321 in the handbook for more homophones.)

Word Sorts ● Have students go through each week's list, grouping words that share a common feature. Students could also explain why other words in the list do not share the feature. (It helps if the students copy the words onto small pieces of paper, so they can physically move them into groups.) Finally, they may write down other words they can think of that share the same feature.

Prefix and Suffix Work ● Provide students with a limited number of prefixes and suffixes. Then ask them to create as many new words as possible by adding these affixes to selected words in the weekly spelling lists. (See pages 217-220 in the handbook for some common prefixes and suffixes.)

Board Work ● Display two or three of the most challenging words from the week's list on the board during a class period. Announce that the words will be erased at the end of the period, and students must try to spell them on a slip of paper before dismissal.

Proofreading Practice ● Ask students to circle two to four words that they think may be misspelled in their writing. Have them check and correct these words before they write a final draft. (Have students keep track of words they continue to misspell in personal spelling dictionaries. See page 228 in the handbook.)

Word Searching ● Have students identify words in their own writing and reading material that follow the pattern for the weekly spelling list.

Last Letter Rules ● Give student teams the same word to spell. Each team member takes a turn adding a letter until the whole word is spelled. The student who adds the last letter rules on the accuracy of the word.

Specialized Spelling ● Ask students to list (and spell correctly) words related to special areas of interest like baseball or the solar system. (Students could create their own specialized dictionaries.)

Plastic Play ● Provide individuals or teams of students with plastic or magnetic letters to practice spelling the words on their weekly list.

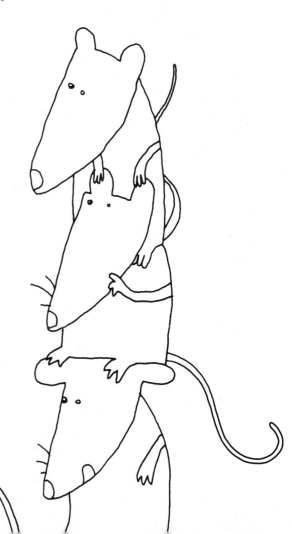

Minilessons

The following pages contain more than 145 minilessons that you and your students can use with the *Write on Track* handbook. These minilessons cover the important skills, strategies, and topics addressed in the handbook.

Minilessons

The Process of Writing

"There's nothing I like better . . . !" All About Writing

■ **READ** page 11 in your handbook. It tells how one student feels about writing.
  Now **WRITE** a few sentences that tell how you feel about writing. You can write whatever you want to. Be honest!

Following the Dotted Line .... All About Writing

■ **OPEN** your handbook to pages 12 and 13. After you read these pages, **LIST** the five steps in the writing process. (To find the five steps, follow the dotted lines from one heading to the next.)
  Then **WRITE** one sentence about each step.

My Day at the Derby .... One Writer's Process

■ **PRACTICE** your revising skills by making some new word choices. **REPLACE** the missing words in the second paragraph of Peter's story about the pinewood derby on page 17 in your handbook. **USE** your own words to make this "your" story.

In the pinewood derby, they have _____

races. Every car gets to race more than once. I didn't win

the first time. In the second race, my car took off like

_____ ! And before I could say

"_____," I won! I was so _____ .

By Peter .... One Writer's Process

▨ **READ** the chapter called "One Writer's Process." It begins on page 14 in your handbook. Then **COMPLETE** the following sentences by adding one or two ideas. Use your own paper and your own words.

1. During prewriting, Peter _picked a subject and collected details_ .

2. When Peter wrote his first draft, he _____ .

3. When Peter revised his draft, he _____ .

4. During editing and proofreading, Peter _____ .

5. When Peter published his story, he _____ .

From Top to Bottom ....Traits of Good Writing

▨ **CHOOSE** an interesting family member or friend to describe. (Or use a picture of someone from a magazine or newspaper.)
   ORGANIZE your writing by describing the person's face (top). Then work your way down.
   WRITE your description so your reader "sees" the person from head to toe.

Computer Personality .... Traits of Good Writing

▨ **READ** the six points that the computer explains about itself on page 23 in your handbook.
   Now **GIVE** the computer a new voice. **DECIDE** whether your computer will be a cattle rancher, an astronaut, a banker, a salesperson, or some other character of your choice. Then **REWRITE** two or three of the six points in words that will make the computer's new voice loud and clear.

Getting to Know PC .... Writing with a Computer

▨ **TURN** to page 23 in your handbook. **STUDY** the computer pictured on this page.
   Then **COVER UP** the names of the different parts; see if you can name the parts just by looking at the picture.

The Name Game .... Writing with a Computer

■ **OPEN** your handbook to page 26. Have your teacher or a parent show you where to put your fingers on the "home row" of the keyboard. **PRACTICE** keyboarding your name until you can do it quickly.

Title Time .... Planning Portfolios

■ **REVIEW** your portfolio. **LOOK** at the titles of your pieces of writing. **REMEMBER** that a title is the first thing a reader sees.
TRY some new titles—ones that rhyme, sound like a tongue twister, ask a question, hook the reader's curiosity, sound like a newspaper headline, and so on.

Saving the Best .... Planning Portfolios

■ **READ** page 28 in your handbook.
NAME one of your favorite pieces of writing.
Then **WRITE** a few sentences explaining why you might want to save it in a portfolio.

Good News, Bad News .... Choosing a Subject

■ **TURN** to page 35 in your handbook and **READ** number 3. Then **START** a list of your bests, worsts, and favorites in a writing notebook or folder.
KEEP adding ideas during the year.

The Road of Life .... Choosing a Subject

■ **OPEN** your handbook to page 34.
STUDY the sample life map. **PLAN** your own life map by listing events you would like to include on it. You may have to ask your parents for help with early events.
Then **DECIDE** how you would like your map to look. (Later, you can draw your map for a classroom display.)

5 × W = 5 W's..................................Gathering Details

- **READ** page 37 in your handbook.
  THINK of an experience you would like to write about. **WRITE** it at the top of a sheet of paper.
  On the same sheet, **LIST** the 5 W's: Who? What? When? Where? and Why? **SKIP** two lines between each question.
  Then **ANSWER** each question about your experience.

Point by Point.....................................Gathering Details

- **READ** page 37 in your handbook.
  LIST the words *subject, purpose, form, audience,* and *voice* on a separate piece of paper.
  WRITE down the five key points for a subject of your choice—a personal story, a play, a poem, a report, or so on. **USE** the sample in the handbook as a guide.

Starting with a Bang.....................Writing a First Draft

- **TURN** to page 38 in your handbook and **READ** "Write Your Beginning." Then **FIND** two beginnings in the handbook samples that you really like. (See pages 83, 99, 141, 150, and 158.)
  SHARE your discoveries with a classmate. **EXPLAIN** why you like each one.

The Most Exciting . . ..Writing a First Draft

- **ASK** a classmate, "What is the most exciting thing you have ever seen or done?"
  WRITE down your classmate's answer.
  Next **CHOOSE** part of the answer that would make a good quotation for the beginning of a story.
  WRITE your quotation using quotation marks and your classmate's name. (See page 38 in your handbook for a sample quotation.)

Off the Subject .... Revising Your Writing

■ **UNDERLINE** the parts of the following paragraph that are off the subject. Everything in this paragraph should relate to the subject— a ruddy duck.

A male ruddy duck is reddish brown. His head is black with big white cheek patches. His bill is blue! I once had a pet duck named Willie. He had an orange bill. My favorite thing about a ruddy duck is his stubby black tail. It makes him look like a little tugboat floating among the cattails in the marsh.

Show Me! .... Revising Your Writing

■ **READ** page 44 in your handbook.
Then **REWRITE** each of the following sentences so they "show" instead of "tell."

1. My neighbor is old.
  <u>My neighbor has white hair and a wrinkled face</u> .

2. We were happy.

3. We were sad.

4. Our classroom is interesting.

First You, Then Me .... Working with Partners

■ **REVIEW** the chapter called "Working with Partners." It begins on page 46 in your handbook.
PRETEND that your teacher has asked you to write a poem about a topic related to summertime. **HELP** a partner decide what to write about. Also **HELP** your partner think of some good words to use in his or her poem.
Then **TRADE** jobs. **ASK** your partner to help you—but this time pretend you are writing a silly poem.

What I Like .... Working with Partners

■ **SELECT** a piece of writing from your portfolio. **READ** it aloud to a partner.

> Then **ASK** your partner to tell you what he or she liked about your writing. For now, focus on all the good things about the writing.
> Now **TRADE** places. **LISTEN** for good things as your partner reads a piece of writing to you.

Editor in Chief .... Editing and Proofreading

■ **READ** the "Editing and Proofreading" checklist on page 51 in your handbook.

> **WORK** with a partner to **PROOFREAD** the draft on page 15, looking for spelling errors. Write both the misspelled words and their correct spellings on a piece of paper. (Normally, you would not proofread a first draft. This is just to help you practice your proofreading skills.)

Two-Headed Editor .... Editing and Proofreading

■ **SELECT** an editing partner. (Each of you should have a piece of writing ready.) Now **OPEN** your handbooks to page 51.

> **USE** the "Editing and Proofreading" checklist to edit your own work while your partner does the same. Then exchange papers and check each other's writing for any missed errors.

Last Step, the Best Step .... Publishing Your Writing

■ **REVIEW** the chapter called "Publishing Your Writing." It starts on page 52 in your handbook.

> **LIST** the different ways you have published your own writing.
> Then **WRITE DOWN** one or two new publishing ideas that you would like to try.
> **SHARE** your ideas with a classmate.

Group Authors .... Publishing Your Writing

■ **PLAN** a publishing project with a small group of classmates. You could make a book that includes a story by each group member. Or you could all perform one story or poem. It's up to your group.

  REVIEW "Five Great Publishing Ideas" on pages 53-55 in your handbook for help.

Topic Sentences .... Writing Paragraphs

■ **READ** pages 58 and 59 in your handbook. Pay special attention to the part about topic sentences at the top of page 59.

  Now **TURN** to the sample paragraphs on pages 60-63. Read the topic sentence for each one.

  On your own paper, **WRITE** the subject and the focus for each topic sentence. The first one has been done for you.

	subject	focus
page 60, "The Funny Dance"	my dog Murphy	danced with Dad

Types of Paragraphs .... Writing Paragraphs

■ **REVIEW** pages 60-63 in your handbook.

  Then **MATCH** each type of paragraph with the correct description listed below.

  Types of Paragraphs

  _____ **1.** expository **a.** tells a story

  _____ **2.** narrative **b.** explains something

  _____ **3.** descriptive **c.** tries to get readers to agree

  _____ **4.** persuasive **d.** describes a person, place, or thing

"Amazing Hawks" .... Writing a Summary

▪ **REVIEW** pages 66-69 in your handbook. Now **TURN** to page 141 and **READ** the student sample report.

   LIST the main ideas that you find in the report. (You'll find four to six.) The ideas in your list could be used to write a summary.

   SHARE your list with a classmate.

Smelly Business .... Writing a Summary

▪ **READ** the sample on page 249 in your handbook. Then **LIST** the main ideas that you find in this writing. If you need help, **TURN** to page 68.

   Special Challenge: **WRITE** a summary of "Skunks," using the ideas in your list.

Sentence Tag .... Writing Basic Sentences

▪ **REVIEW** page 72 in your handbook.

   WRITE this sentence at the top of a sheet of paper: I play tag.

   Then **REWRITE** the sentence using a different subject. **ASK** a partner to rewrite the sentence with still another subject. Next, **REWRITE** the sentence using a different verb. (You may change other words, too.)

   KEEP trading back and forth, writing sentences with different subjects and predicates. **ADD** describing words to make your sentences even more fun.

   Example Sentences:

   Tim plays tag. (different subject)

   My sister plays tag. (different subject)

   My sister wins at tag! (different verb)

   My silly sister likes tackle tag.

   (describing words plus different verb)

Neat and Complete .... Writing Basic Sentences

■ **REVIEW** the information on sentence fragments on page 73 in your handbook. Then on your own paper, **MAKE** each fragment below into a complete sentence.

1. After the rain.   <u>We collected worms after the rain.</u>

2. Worked before lunch.   **4.** Stayed overnight.

3. At the mall.   **5.** With my best friend.

And then . . . And then . . . . Combining Sentences

■ **WRITE** about something you did during recess. **USE** a lot of *and*'s in your writing. (Joe ran out for a pass and waved his arms and yelled and then . . .)

SWITCH papers with a partner and **CORRECT** each other's rambling ideas. **READ** about rambling sentences on page 73 and "Four Ways to Combine Sentences" on page 75 in your handbook for help.

Let's eat! .... Combining Sentences

■ **WRITE** three sentences describing your favorite food. Then **COMBINE** all three sentences into one sentence. **LOOK** at "Use a Series" on page 75 in your handbook.

The Forms of Writing

My Life! .... Writing in Journals

■ **READ** pages 77-78 in your handbook.
Then **WRITE** the first entry in your own personal journal. **WRITE** about something you saw, something you did, or something you heard about. Don't worry about spelling every word right. Just get all of your ideas on paper.

Two R's: Readin' and Writin' .... Writing in Journals

■ **READ** page 79 in your handbook. Now **TURN** to page 260 and **READ** the story "Walking Catfish."
WRITE a few sentences telling what you think about this story. This could be the beginning of your own reading journal.

A Pet's Album .... Making Albums

---

■ **SELECT** a pet (cat, dog, turtle, bird, etc.).
LIST the types of things this pet might collect in an album.
PLAN the pages for the pet's album.

Tabby & Me .... Making Albums

■ **OPEN** your handbook to pages 80 and 81. **SELECT** a subject for a pet or special-person album. (If you make an album about a person, you could give it to him or her as a special gift.)
MAKE some notes about what you would put in the album.
USE the suggestions on page 81 for ideas.

Possum Tale .... Writing Personal Narratives

---

■ A personal narrative answers the question "Guess what happened?"
READ the personal narrative on page 83 in your handbook.
Then **WRITE** two sentences that tell what happened.
SHARE your sentences with a classmate.

Strange Happenings .... Writing Personal Narratives

On a sheet of paper, **LIST** the words *happy, funny, proud, strange,* and *important*.

Under each word, **WRITE** one or two things that happened to you. (List happy experiences under the word "happy," and so on.)

When you finish, **ASK,** *"Which of these happenings would my classmates be most interested in?"*

Then **ASK,** *"Which of the interesting events do I remember the most about?"* This final choice would probably make a good personal narrative. For writing guidelines, see pages 84-85 in your handbook.

Collecting Ideas .... Writing Lists

READ "Collecting Ideas for Writing" on page 87 in your handbook.

On a sheet of paper, **NAME** your favorite or your worst day of the week. **LIST** different words that come to mind when you think of this day.

SHARE your list with a classmate, and **SAVE** it in a notebook or folder. Sometime you might want to write a "day" story or poem.

Happy Thoughts to You! .... Writing Lists

READ page 88 in your handbook.

Then **MAKE** your own "happy list." Keep your list in an idea notebook, a writing folder, or a journal. (You may want to work on this with a partner.)

Apples for the Teacher................ Writing Friendly Notes

Years ago, one way a student showed a teacher appreciation was to give the teacher an apple.

DRAW the shape of an apple on a piece of paper.

WRITE a short note to your teacher, sharing a friendly thought. See pages 90-93 in your handbook if you need help.

Notes to You! .... Writing Friendly Notes

■ **REVIEW** "Writing Friendly Notes" on pages 90-93 in your handbook.
   It gives four reasons to send notes. **PICK** a reason to send a note.
   Then **WRITE** a note to someone in your class. Ask the person to
   write back!

Custodians and Secretaries ..... Writing Friendly Letters

■ **WRITE** a friendly letter to someone on the staff of your school. You
   could write a friendly greeting to a teacher's aide, librarian, school
   secretary, or principal.
   USE the proper form for a friendly letter shown on page 95 in your
   handbook.

Five-Part Harmony .... Writing Friendly Letters

■ Carefully **REVIEW** pages 94-95 in your handbook. Then **CLOSE** your
   handbook and look at the list of words below. They are the parts of a
   friendly letter, but they are in the wrong order. **REWRITE** the list in
   the right order. **OPEN** your handbook to check your work.

   1. body   3. signature   5. heading
   2. closing   4. salutation

Animal Families .... Writing Family Stories

■ Many animals live in families similar to human families.
   WRITE a short family story that may have happened in your
   family. However, write the story as though you were a family of
   farm animals, forest animals, or zoo animals.

All in the Family .... Writing Family Stories

■ **OPEN** your handbook to pages 98-99. **READ** about family stories.
   Now **USE** the ideas listed on page 100 under "Read and
   Remember" to help you list possible subjects for your own family
   story. Select the best idea from your list for a story.

Knowing Your A's and B's .... Writing Alphabet Books

■ **PRETEND** that your teacher has asked you to write an alphabet book about different countries.

> On your own paper, **LIST** a country for each of the first five letters of the alphabet. The maps in your handbook on pages 367-376 will be a big help.
>
> **ADD** an interesting fact if you know one. (See the example below and the student samples on page 104 in your handbook.)

A ___ustralia is a huge island known for its kangaroos___ .

Getting a Little Crazy! .... Writing Alphabet Books

■ **STUDY** page 107 in your handbook. Then **START** a zany alphabet book about food, geography, or creepy crawlers.

> **WRITE** at least four or five lines. **SHARE** your work.
>
> **KEEP** going if you like the start of your ABC book.

Getting Down to Basics ...... Writing Newspaper Stories

■ On a sheet of paper, list the 5 W's *(who? what? when? where? and why?)*.

> **FIND** the answers to the 5 W's in a story in your school or local newspaper.
>
> **WRITE** the answers in your own words. To show you how it's done, we've answered the 5 W's for the sample news story on page 109 in your handbook.

Who?	the students in Ms. Grayson's class
What?	collected 22,000 aluminum cans
When?	in six weeks
Where?	mostly from their parents
Why?	to raise money to buy trees for their school yard

In My Opinion .... Writing Newspaper Stories

■ **READ** and **DISCUSS** the letter to the editor on page 113 in your handbook.

Then **LIST** three topics you would like to talk about in this type of letter.

SHARE your ideas with your classmates.

The Big Three .... Writing Book Reviews

■ **REVIEW** pages 114-116 in your handbook.

On a piece of paper, **WRITE** the title of the last book you read.

ANSWER one of the three questions at the top of page 116 about this book. **USE** at least two or three sentences.

SHARE your answer with a classmate.

Words About Books .... Writing Book Reviews

■ **STUDY** the list of words on page 119 in your handbook.

Then **CLOSE** your handbook and explain each word listed below. When you finish, **OPEN** your handbook to check your work.

1. Dialogue is the talking between characters .

2. Fiction _____ .

3. The plot _____ .

4. The setting _____ .

Robotics ....How-To Writing

■ Many things are run by computers today. **READ** about Roberto's homework machine on page 125 in your handbook.

WRITE a set of directions for a robot that can do things for you at your house or in your school.

Left at the Stoplight .... How-To Writing

■ **WRITE** directions from your classroom to another part of your school. You could explain how to get to the playground, lunchroom, or library.
> **WRITE** your directions in a list like the one at the bottom of page 124 in your handbook.
> **ASK** a classmate to check your work by testing your directions.

Why Write? .... Writing Business Letters

■ **REVIEW** pages 126-127 in your handbook.
> **THINK** of a business letter you would like to write. Do you need or want information about something? Do you have a problem to solve?
> **WRITE** a sentence that tells what information you need, or what problem you have to solve.

And the Envelope, Please ...... Writing Business Letters

■ **ADDRESS** an envelope to the president. (Put your return address on the envelope, too.)
> **LOOK** at page 133 in your handbook to make sure you do everything right. Here is the president's address: The President of the United States, The White House, 1600 Pennsylvania Avenue, Washington, DC 20500.

Getting Started .... Writing Classroom Reports

■ **REVIEW** pages 135-137 in your handbook.
> **CHOOSE** a subject for a classroom report.
> On a sheet of paper, **WRITE** at least four questions about your subject that you would like to answer. Remember to write questions that can't be answered with a yes or no.

Getting a Grip on a Grid .... Writing Classroom Reports

▓ **TURN** to page 138 in your handbook and study the gathering grid. Then **MAKE** your own grid to use for a classroom report. **LEAVE** enough space for at least four questions and three sources of information.
Tip: Use a big piece of paper for your work.

Before, During, After .... Writing Photo Essays

▓ **FIND** a picture in an old magazine of something happening with people or animals.
WRITE a sentence (a caption) that tells what you think is happening in the picture.
If you have time, **DRAW** what you think happened before this scene and after this scene. Then **WRITE** a caption for each of those drawings.

Photo Shoot .... Writing Photo Essays

▓ **REVIEW** "Writing Photo Essays" on pages 142-147 in your handbook.
THINK of a person or an animal that would make a good subject for this type of writing.
On your own paper, **MAKE** a list of three or more photos you would like to take of this subject. We've started a list of photo ideas for a circus clown.

1. photo showing clown putting on makeup
2. photo showing clown's foot next to huge clown shoe

At the End .... Writing Realistic Stories

▓ **READ** about realistic stories on pages 149-150 in your handbook.
Then **THINK** of a funny, exciting, or important event in your life.
WRITE a different ending for this experience. **SHARE** your ideas with a classmate.

You Don't Say .... Writing Realistic Stories

■ **THINK** of a funny, exciting, or important event in your life. (It could be the same one you used in the last minilesson.)
    WRITE at least four lines of dialogue between two characters in your story. For help, **STUDY** the model on page 150 in your handbook.

Way Back When .... Writing Time-Travel Fantasies

■ **READ** pages 154-155 about time-travel fantasies in your handbook.
    PRETEND your teacher asked you to write a fantasy about some time in the past. **DECIDE** which time you'd like to visit.
    WRITE down two or three facts that you know about this time.
    SHARE your work with a classmate.

A Problem in Time .... Writing Time-Travel Fantasies

■ Every good story needs a problem! **READ** the fantasy on pages 158-159 in your handbook to see what we mean by a problem.
    PRETEND that you've decided to write a time-travel fantasy that takes place in outer space.
    WRITE one or two sentences describing a problem you could put in your story.

Play Along .... Writing Plays

■ **REVIEW** pages 160-163 in your handbook about writing plays.
    CHOOSE a story that you could turn into a play.
    Now **LIST** the *story events*. Page 163 shows you how.

Talk! Talk! Talk! .... Writing Plays

■ To practice writing dialogue for a play, **WRITE** Scene 2 for the sample in the handbook (page 161). Scene 2 is described on page 163.
    WORK on this activity with a classmate if you like.

"When I Grow Up" .... Writing Free-Verse Poetry

■ **READ** Kristen Murphy's free-verse poem on page 170 in your handbook.
WRITE the start of your own "When I Grow Up" poem. **INCLUDE**
at least four things you would like to be.

Making Comparisons .... Writing Free-Verse Poetry

■ **READ** about making comparisons on page 173 in your handbook.
FIND one example of a simile or a metaphor and one example of
personification in poems in your reading book.
SHARE your discoveries with a classmate.

Detective Poems .... Traditional and Playful Poetry

■ Be a detective and a poet. **WRITE** a 5-W's poem. **ANSWER** the five
questions: *who? what? when? where?* and *why?* See the bottom of page
178 in your handbook.
Then **READ** lines 2-5 for a partner or the class. It is a riddle. Can
your listeners guess the "who" of your poem?

All Decked Out .... Traditional and Playful Poetry

■ **READ** about cinquain poetry on page 175 in your handbook.
Then **WRITE** a *cinquain* about a favorite piece of clothing.
USE the sample in your handbook as a guide.
SHARE your results.

The Tools of Learning

One Way or Another............................Using the Library

■ **REVIEW** pages 181-184 in your handbook. Then **FIND OUT** if your school library uses a card catalog or a computer catalog.

On a half sheet of paper, **LIST** two or three important things the handbook says about the type of catalog used in your school. **SHARE** your ideas with your classmates.

Parts of a Book................................Using the Library

■ In your classroom or library, **FIND** a reference book.

Then **OPEN** your handbook to "Understanding the Parts of a Book" on page 187.

FIND as many of these parts as you can in the book you selected.

Emoticons................................Using the Internet

■ **SHARE** your favorite emoticon (symbol made using keyboard characters) with the class.

DISCUSS how you use emoticons to add feelings to your e-mail messages. :)

Challenge: Try inventing some new emoticons.

Picture Talk................................Reading Graphics

■ **STUDY** page 196 in your handbook. Then **THINK** of another symbol you know about.

DRAW this symbol. (If you can't think of one, create a new symbol.) **SHARE** your drawing with your classmates.

On the Table .... Reading Graphics

▪ **STUDY** page 199 in your handbook.
Then, as a class, **MAKE** your own table. Your table could tell about your favorite pets, your favorite football teams, or your favorite foods. **DRAW** a copy of your table on a large piece of paper.

Working on New Words .... Reading New Words

▪ **REVIEW** pages 200-201 in your handbook and **PUT** a bookmark by these pages.
Then **READ** about commercials on page 234. **USE** the strategies on pages 200-201 to help you read any new words.
TALK about your reading with your classmates.

Smelly Skunks .... Reading to Understand

▪ **REVIEW** page 204 in your handbook. Then **MAKE** your own KWL chart. On the line for the title, write "Skunks." **FILL IN** the *know* and *want* columns of your chart with ideas and questions you have about skunks. Now **READ** "Skunks" on page 249 and **FILL IN** the *learn* column of your chart.

Mapping .... Reading to Understand

▪ **STUDY** the sample reading map on page 205 of your handbook.
Now **READ** "Amazing Hawks" on page 141. **MAKE** a reading map of this report. Begin with the word *hawks* in a circle. One of your main ideas could be *eating habits* or *food*.

Word Search .... Building Vocabulary Skills

▪ **TURN** to page 231 in your handbook. **CHOOSE** a new word on this page to add to your vocabulary. **LOOK UP** the word in a dictionary.
LIST three different types of information about the word (*meaning, history, synonyms,* and so on). See pages 212-213 if you're not sure how to use a dictionary.

Just the Right Word .... Building Vocabulary Skills

▪ **LOOK UP** the word *run* in a thesaurus. **FIND** three synonyms for it.
   WRITE a sentence using each one. Make sure each sentence is
   different. See page 214 if you're not sure how to use a
   thesaurus.

Un-lock-*ed* .... Using Prefixes, Suffixes, Roots

▪ In 5 minutes, **LIST** as many real words as you can that use the prefix
   un- and as many real words as you can that use the suffix *-ed*.
   Challenge: List as many words as you can that use both the prefix
   un- and the suffix *-ed* in the same word (*unlocked, uncovered,*
   unmarked, and so on)!

First Cousins .... Becoming a Better Speller

▪ **READ** the first paragraph on page 226 in your handbook. It lists some
   word relatives of the word *night*.
   On a sheet of paper, **WRITE** the word *rain*.
   Then **WRITE** as many word relatives of *rain* as you can.
      CHECK the list of suffixes on pages 219-220 for ideas.
   SHARE your words with a classmate.

By the Rules .... Becoming a Better Speller

▪ **REVIEW** the four basic spelling rules on pages 228-229 in your
   handbook.
      THINK of at least one word that fits each rule. (Don't use the
      words in the handbook.) **SHARE** your words with your
      classmates.

Seeing the World........................... Learning to View

▪ **REVIEW** page 233 in your handbook. In the first paragraph, **LOOK** over the list of things you can see on television specials.

THINK of one person, place, or thing you saw on television that you have never seen in person.

WRITE a few sentences about it. *What do you remember most? What did you learn? What did you like or not like about the program?*

Storytelling............................. Learning to Listen

▪ **READ** the listening tips on page 237 in your handbook.

Then **LISTEN** carefully while a classmate tells you a personal story.

RETELL the story in as much detail as you can.

ASK your partner how well you did. When you finish, **SWITCH** roles.

Speaking Parts .... Performing Poems

▪ **TEAM UP** with one or two classmates.

SCRIPT one of the poems in the handbook. **OPEN** your handbook to page 240 for a sample script.

You could also **SCORE** the poem, using the sample on page 241 as a guide.

Talk Topic.......................... Giving Short Talks

▪ **READ** the top of page 245 in your handbook.

Then **LIST** these three headings on a piece of paper: *Something that happened to me, Something I like to do, Something I read about.* **SKIP** about four lines between each one.

WRITE two or three topics under each heading. **SHARE** your list with a classmate. Then **SELECT** the best topic for a short talk.

Dream Job .... Learning to Interview

▓ **READ** page 252 in your handbook.

Then **WRITE** at the top of a piece of paper what kind of work you would like to do when you grow up.

LIST three or four questions you would ask someone who knows about this job. **DECIDE** who could answer these questions for you.

SHARE your list with your classmates.

Story Cards .... Telling Stories

▓ **REVIEW** pages 257-259 in your handbook. Then **TURN** to page 150 and **READ** "A Very Far Hit."

WRITE one note card for the first line in the story and another note card for the last line.

Then **WRITE** note cards for each important event between the beginning and the end. **SHARE** your work with a classmate.

Circling Around Subjects ...... Using Graphic Organizers

▓ **REVIEW** page 266 in your handbook. Then **THINK** of two animals that are alike in some ways.

MAKE a Venn diagram comparing these animals. You can use information you know, or you can read about the animals in a reference book.

Trouble, Trouble .... Thinking Clearly

▓ Do this minilesson with a partner. **PRETEND** that you are at the playground with a friend. You find a dog that can't get up. You want to help, but you don't know what to do. No one else is at the playground.

FOLLOW the directions on page 269 to solve this problem.

WRITE down your ideas for numbers 1-4 on this page.

SHARE your work with your classmates.

Logging It .... Writing to Learn

- **REVIEW** "Writing to Learn" on pages 274-275 in your handbook.
  Then **WRITE** a few sentences or draw a few pictures that explain
  something you just learned in math.

Working Smart .... Completing Assignments

- **THINK** about how you complete assignments.
  Then **READ** page 278 in your handbook. **LIST** two or three new
  things you will try the next time you study. **COMPARE** lists
  with your classmates.

Surprise! .... Working in Groups

- With a partner, **READ** pages 280-281 in your handbook.
  Then **PLAN** a pretend party for someone you both know and like.
  FILL OUT a "group plan" like the one on page 283.

Short Answer .... Taking Tests

- **REVIEW** page 290 in your handbook.
  THINK about a subject you are studying in science.
  WRITE DOWN some ideas for a short-answer question about the
  subject.
  As a class, **SHARE** your ideas and **DECIDE** on one good question.
  Then **PLAN** and **WRITE** your answer following the tips on page
  290.

Proofreader's Guide

I love cookies. .... Marking Punctuation

WRITE a paragraph about your favorite food. Write at least four sentences.
LEAVE OUT the periods at the end of your sentences.
Then **TRADE** paragraphs with a partner.
PUT periods where they are needed in each other's paragraph.

Hungry Mungry Monkey .... Marking Punctuation

PRETEND you are going to write a story about a family of monkeys.
MAKE UP a last name for the family. Also **MAKE UP** first names and middle names for each of the monkeys.
WRITE the full names. Then **WRITE** the names using first and middle initials.

Catfish are smooth, shiny, and slippery! .... Marking Punctuation

WRITE a sentence using three words to describe an alligator.
PUT commas where they are needed.
Now **WRITE** sentences about two other animals.
USE three describing words in each sentence. Don't forget the commas!

Don't forget contractions! .... Marking Punctuation

OPEN your handbook to page 299. **STUDY** the section on using apostrophes in contractions. Now **CLOSE** your handbook.
WRITE the contractions of the following words. **TURN** to page 299 to check your work.

1. you are
2. do not
3. it is
4. they are
5. is not
6. was not

The Poem "True Blue" .... Marking Punctuation

▓ **TURN** to page 300 in your handbook. **REVIEW** the section "To Punctuate Titles."

Now **TURN** to the chapter "Writing Free-Verse Poetry," which begins on page 167.

On your own paper, **WRITE** the names of the sample poems in this chapter. **USE** quotation marks correctly.

Spelling It Out .... Checking Mechanics

▓ **TURN** to page 310 in your handbook. **STUDY** the section "Acronyms." Then **WRITE** the acronyms for the following phrases:

_____ **1.** Rainforest Action Network

_____ **2.** Performing Animal Welfare Society

_____ **3.** Handicapped Equestrian Learning Program

_____ **4.** North Atlantic Treaty Organization

_____ **5.** Cooperative (for) American Relief Everywhere

_____ **6.** Mothers Against Drunk Driving

_____ **7.** National Aeronautics (and) Space Administration

Words or Numerals? .... Checking Mechanics

▓ **STUDY** page 309 in your handbook. Then **FILL IN** the blanks in the following sentences.

WRITE either "words" or "numerals," whichever is correct. **TURN** to page 309 to check your work.

1. Write numbers that begin a sentence as _____ .

2. Write numbers that are less than 10 as _____ .

3. Write numbers that are greater than 10 as _____ .

4. Write very large numbers as _____ and _____ .

5. Write numbers in dates, times, and addresses as _____ .

6. Write numbers that are amounts of money as _____ .

Mail from AL to WY .... Checking Mechanics

■ **OPEN** your handbook to page 311. On the chart of state abbreviations, **LOOK UP** the postal abbreviations for the following places:

_____ 1. Texas

_____ 2. New York

_____ 3. Florida

_____ 4. Utah

_____ 5. Michigan

_____ 6. California

_____ 7. District of Columbia

_____ 8. West Virginia

_____ 9. Kansas

_____ 10. Indiana

_____ 11. Connecticut

_____ 12. Mississippi

Another Name .... Checking Mechanics

■ **OPEN** your handbook to page 307, "Geographic Names."
For each type of name listed (planets and heavenly bodies, continents, and so on), **LIST** another example. Do as many as you can on your own. **CHECK** a map or an atlas if you need help.

Hidden Names ....Checking Your Spelling

■ **LOOK** for boys' and girls' names within the following words from the "Checking Your Spelling" list on pages 312-315 in your handbook.

Example: <u>lou</u>d is Lou and <u>flo</u>or is Flo

Boys' Names

1. asleep
2. August
3. early
4. half
5. March
6. probably
7. scared
8. toward

Girls' Names

9. April
10. bear
11. better
12. December
13. January
14. join
15. maybe
16. truth

The Other Half .... Checking Your Spelling

■ **WRITE** the homophone for each of the following words from "Checking Your Spelling" on pages 312-315 in your handbook. **TURN** to "Using the Right Word" on pages 316-321 to check your work.

1. aunt   **3.** dear   **5.** know   **7.** past   **9.** their

2. would   **4.** knew   **6.** piece   **8.** through   **10.** you're

Special Challenge: Find more homophones in the spelling list.

Rhyming Lists .... Checking Your Spelling

■ **MAKE** lists of rhyming words using the list of spelling words on pages 312-315 in your handbook.

ADD words to the two lists below:

aught/ought words	ight words
caught	right
bought	

Now **WRITE** a rhyming list poem. See pages 171-173. **USE** the words from your lists.

Children catch . . . . Checking Your Spelling

■ **FIND** the "Checking Your Spelling" list in your handbook (pages 312-315). **CHOOSE** one letter of the alphabet. Then **WRITE** a sentence using as many of the words listed under that letter as you can.

It's time to give the turtle its food. .... Using the Right Word

■ *Its* is a pronoun. (*Remember:* A pronoun is a word that takes the place of a noun.) *It's* is a contraction that stands for "it is."

WRITE two sentences. In one sentence, use *its* correctly. In your other sentence, use *it's* correctly. If you need help, see page 318 in your handbook. (Or just **CHECK OUT** the title of this minilesson!)

Their portfolios aren't there. ...... Using the Right Word

Their is a pronoun. It takes the place of a noun. *There* is an adverb that tells *where*.

WRITE two sentences. In one sentence, use *their* correctly. In your other sentence, use *there* correctly. If you need help, see page 320 in your handbook. (Or just **CHECK OUT** the title of this minilesson.)

"I won another one!" .... Using the Right Word

FILL IN the blanks in the sentences below using *one* or *won* correctly. **CHECK** page 319 in your handbook for help.

1. I ____won____ two hamsters at the picnic.

2. My dad said I could only keep _____ .

3. "But, Dad!" I said. "I _____ them!"

4. "Sorry," he said. "You have to give _____ away."

5. So I gave _____ to my friend Samantha.

6. Samantha's mom told me, "Stacy, I wish you had _____ two cakes instead of two hamsters!"

My Favorite Movie .... Understanding Sentences

On your own paper, **TURN** the following sentence fragment into a complete sentence:

My favorite movie.

Example: My favorite movie is Pocahontas.

Now **TURN** your complete sentence into a run-on sentence by adding another complete thought to it.

Example: My favorite movie is Pocahontas I really like the music.

Finally, **CORRECT** your run-on sentence.

Example: My favorite movie is Pocahontas. I really like the music.

Just the Facts.......................... Understanding Sentences

WRITE sentence fragments that give facts about people in your class. Write two fragments that need a verb. (*Example:* Last summer, Kirsten.) Write two fragments that need a subject. (*Example:* Has a pet snake.)
TRADE with a partner. Try to turn each other's fragments into correct, complete sentences.

Simple or Compound? ....Understanding Sentences

GET OUT an old story or report you have written.
PICK OUT all of the simple and compound sentences. (See page 325 in your handbook to review simple and compound sentences.)
WRITE an S at the beginning of each simple sentence.
WRITE a C at the beginning of each compound sentence.

Sentence Detectives .... Understanding Sentences

TURN to page 249 in your handbook.
READ the student sample "Skunks." **FIND** one example of each kind of sentence—declarative, interrogative, imperative, and exclamatory—in this writing. (Page 325 in your handbook explains the different kinds of sentences.) This is a good activity to do with a partner.

Finding Subjects and Predicates .... Understanding Sentences

CHOOSE an old story or report you have written.
In each of your sentences, **UNDERLINE** the simple subject once and the simple predicate twice. (See handbook pages 323-325.) Things to remember:
1. Compound sentences will have two subjects and two predicates.
2. Some simple sentences may have a compound subject, a compound verb, or both.

Put a stop to run-ons! .... Understanding Sentences

■ **CHOOSE** a paragraph from one of your favorite books or stories. **TURN** some of the sentences into run-on sentences. (See page 73 in your handbook for an explanation.)

TRADE papers with a partner. **CORRECT** each other's run-ons by turning each one into two correct sentences.

Finally, **COMPARE** your corrected sentences with the sentences in the book or story. (They don't have to be the same, but they do have to be correct.)

Calling All Nouns .... Understanding Our Language

■ **PRACTICE** finding nouns. (Remember, a noun names a person, a place, a thing, or an idea.)

First **TURN** to page 90 in your handbook.

FIND all the nouns in the paragraph "Short and Quick."

On your own paper, **LIST** the nouns. (*Hint:* **Someone** is a pronoun, not a noun. There are nine nouns in all.)

Whose hair? .... Understanding Our Language

■ **TURN** to page 328 in your handbook. **READ** about "Possessive Pronouns."

Then **USE** each of the following possessive pronouns in a sentence. **WRITE** all your sentences about hair.

1. their: _Tracy and Maria wear their hair the same way._

2. your   **3.** my   **4.** our   **5.** his   **6.** her

For the Birds .... Understanding Our Language

■ **TURN** to page 328 in your handbook. **READ** about "Common Personal Pronouns."

Now **TURN** to page 92. **READ** the friendly note under "To Send a Special Message."

LIST all the personal pronouns you find in this note. There are eight of them.

We rode . . . . *Understanding Our Language*

■ **OPEN** your handbook to page 329. **REVIEW** "Types of Verbs." Now **WRITE** three sentences about something your whole class did together. It could be a project or a field trip. In your first sentence, use an action verb. In your second sentence, use a linking verb. In your third sentence, use a helping verb.

It will . . . . *Understanding Our Language*

■ **TURN** to page 58 in your handbook. **READ** "Snow Day!" All the verbs in this paragraph are in the past tense. Now **PRETEND** that you can predict the future. As you read the model aloud, **CHANGE** all the verbs to future tense. (*Hint:* You'll use the word *will* in every sentence.) We've written the first sentence below to get you started.

It will snow a lot tomorrow, so school will let out early.

Quickly or Slowly? .... *Understanding Our Language*

■ **TURN** to page 335 in your handbook. **REVIEW** "Adverbs."
On your own paper, **DRAW** a describing wheel. (If you need to see what a describing wheel looks like, turn to page 265.) The subject of your describing wheel is *run*.
ADD as many adverbs as you can think of. *Remember:* Adverbs can tell *how* something is done, *where* it is done, or *when* it is done.

Preposition Mission .... *Understanding Our Language*

■ **TURN** to page 336 in your handbook. **READ** about "Prepositions." Now **TURN** to page 124. **LOOK AT** "How to Get to My House from School."
FIND the prepositional phrases in the directions. (There are five of them. *After* is used as a conjunction in this case)
WRITE the phrases on your own paper and **CIRCLE** the preposition in each one.

Student Almanac

New and Improved .... Using Language

- **READ** the "New Words" section on page 341 in your handbook.
  LIST two or three inventions that have added words to English.
  THINK of two new words related to each invention, and **WRITE** them next to the correct invention.
  TALK about your ideas with your classmates.

Talking Hands .... Using Language

- **LOOK** at the sign-language chart on page 344 in your handbook.
  MEMORIZE the signs for the letters in your first name. **PRACTICE** them until you can sign your name quickly.

Greetings! .... Using Language

- **TURN** to page 343 in your handbook.
  USE the table to help you give the following greetings in each language.
  1. Hello in Chinese: _____dzău_____
  2. Hello in French: _____
  3. Hello in Farsi: _____
  4. Hello in Spanish: _____
  5. Good-bye in Spanish: _____
  6. Good-bye in Swedish: _____

Speedy Delivery! .... Using Language

- **WRITE** a friendly or funny note in cursive to a classmate. **DROP** it in his or her student mailbox, or **DELIVER** it in person. (Make sure to ask for a note in return.)

Watch! .... Using Language

▪ **SELECT** one letter in the alphabet. **REFER** to page 347 in your
handbook to see how the letter is formed in cursive.
PRACTICE writing this letter at the beginning, in the middle, and
at the end of words. (Make sure you know both the lowercase
and uppercase forms.)
On the board, **SHOW** your classmates how to form this letter in
different positions in words.

Bees Buzzing Backward .... Using Language

▪ **CREATE** a tongue twister using as many *b* words as you can.
MAKE a copy of your twister using your best cursive handwriting.
SHARE your work with a classmate.
Note to Teachers: Create minilessons for other cursive letters
that pose special problems.

Final Check .... Using Language

▪ **WRITE** the final copy of your next writing assignment in cursive.
EVALUATE the quality of your handwriting using the checklist on
page 347 in your handbook as a guide. (If you're not happy with
your work, try again.)

The Geese and Swans
of Puddle Lake .... Exploring Science

▪ **TURN** to the table of animal facts on page 349 in your handbook.
IMAGINE that you are studying ducks, geese, and swans.
On a separate sheet of paper, **LIST** all the different words you
could use for these three birds.

The Bunny and the Calf................... Exploring Science

LOOK at the table of animal facts on page 349 in your handbook. **IMAGINE** that all of the young animals listed on this page went to summer camp together.

WRITE a paragraph describing what some of the animals did at camp. **USE** the correct words for the young of at least four different animals.

Cups, Pints, Quarts .... Exploring Science

TURN to page 352 in your handbook.

USE the list of measurements to help you fill in the blanks below. (Look at the part of the list that gives **capacity** measures.)

1. **2 cups** of orange juice = _____1_____ pint of orange juice

2. **4 cups** of iced tea = _____ pints of iced tea

3. **4 cups** of iced tea = _____ quart of iced tea

4. **16 cups** of milk = _____ pints of milk

5. **16 cups** of milk = _____ quarts of milk

Silly Millimeter .... Exploring Science

OPEN your handbook to page 353.

USE the list of metric measures to help you fill in the blanks below. (Look at the part giving **length** measures.)

1. The letters **mm** stand for _____millimeter_____.

2. The letters **cm** stand for _____.

3. The letter **m** stands for _____.

4. The letters **km** stand for _____.

5. One **kilometer** equals 1,000 _____.

Space Travelers .... Exploring Science

▨ **DO** this minilesson with a partner. Both of you **OPEN** your handbooks to pages 350-351. You're going to take turns asking each other questions about the table.

> **WRITE DOWN** two or three questions for your partner to answer by looking at the table. Below are two sample questions you could ask.

> **1.** Which planet is closest to the sun? _____

> **2.** Which planet has the most moons? _____

X + Y = 17 .... Improving Math Skills

▨ **WRITE** four equations that equal 17.

> **USE** the "Addition and Subtraction Table" on page 359 in your handbook.

> *Challenge:* Which total number on the chart has the most equations?

> If you have a favorite number, write a sentence explaining why it is your favorite.

Roman Numerals for Today .... Improving Math Skills

▨ **ANSWER** the following questions using Roman numerals and the chart on the bottom of page 360 in your handbook.

> How old are you? _____   What year is it? _____

> What month is it? _____   On what day of the month is your birthday? _____   How many people are in your family? _____

Rounding to the Nearest 10 .... Improving Math Skills

▨ **ROUND** the following numbers to the nearest 10.
> **USE** page 361 in your handbook to help you.

> 47   122   6   211   95

Digital Clocks ....Improving Math Skills

■ Have fun with digital times. You may want to look at the clock faces
on page 363 in your handbook.
ANSWER the following questions.

  1. What times use all the same numbers?

  2. What times make you think of airplanes?

  3. What time is an emergency phone number?

  4. Which times seem to use skip-counting?

  Challenge: **MAKE UP** questions for your classmates to answer.

Sharing Borders ....Using Maps

■ **LOOK** at the map of the United States on page 368 in your handbook,
or the regional state maps on pages 369-376, to answer the following
questions.

  1. Which states have no states touching their borders?

  2. Which state has only one state that borders it?

  3. Which states have only two states touching their borders?

  4. Which state has the most other states touching its borders?

  5. How many states border your state?

  Challenge: Write a paragraph about a visit you made to another
  state.

Capital Idea! ....Using Maps

■ **USE** the maps on pages 368-376 in your handbook to answer this
question: Which four states have a capital city whose name begins
with the same letter as the name of the state?
Then **ANSWER** this question: What do you know about the capital
city of your state? Write a letter to the offices of your state
capitol, asking for information about the city. (Ask your teacher
or librarian for the address.)

Name That State...Using Maps

READ about latitude and longitude on page 366 in your handbook.
Then LOOK at the map of the United States on page 368.
WRITE down which state you would be in at each of the following
coordinates:

1. 30 N 100 W

3. 40 N 75 W

2. 45 N 115 W

4. 40 N 90 W

What two coordinates would tell someone which state you live in?

Birds, Beasts, Or?...Using Maps

STUDY the list of state nicknames on pages 378 and 379 in your
handbook. Then answer the following questions:

1. Which two states have bird nicknames?

2. Which three states have animal nicknames?

3. Which state nickname relates to insects?

Challenge: Which seven states have tree nicknames?
What is your state's nickname? What is your favorite state
nickname?

If you have a nickname, write a short story about how you got it.
Maybe it's a well-known family story. If you don't have a
nickname, maybe you wish you had one. Write a paragraph
about a nickname you'd like to have.

Traveling Through History........... History in the Making

OPEN your handbook to the historical time line (pages 382-391).
On your own paper, WRITE down who invented the following:

1. steamboat

3. car

2. bicycle

4. airplane

Also IDENTIFY when each was invented.

The Start of Something Good ... History in the Making

▧ Below are two lists: a list of foods and a list of dates. **DRAW** a line from the food to the date when you think it was invented.
CHECK your work by finding each date on the time line in your handbook (pages 382-391).

1. popcorn   1630

2. hot dogs   1786

3. potato chips   1866

4. ice cream   1900

5. root beer   1925

1850-1900 ....History in the Making

▧ **STUDY** the time line on page 387 in your handbook. **NOTICE** the inventions in "Science & Inventions" listed in 1851, 1876, 1879, 1893, and 1896.
WRITE a short paragraph about a day in your life without one of these important inventions.

50, 75, or 100 Years Ago ....History in the Making

▧ **SELECT** a "U.S. History" event from the time line pages 388-390 in your handbook—something that took place 50 to 100 years ago.
TELL a partner what you think it would have been like to be living at that time.
EXPLAIN how you might have felt when you heard about the event. If your story sounds interesting, **WRITE** it down and keep it in your writing folder for future use.

Minilesson Answer Key

The Process of Writing

Following the Dotted Line (page 206)

Prewriting, Writing, Revising,
Editing and Proofreading, Publishing

By Peter (page 207)

Answers may vary.

2. put all his ideas on paper
3. read his draft and changed different parts
4. made sure his sentences made sense, and he checked for errors
5. shared it with his friends

Off the Subject (page 210)

I once had a pet duck named Willie. He had an orange bill.

Show Me! (page 210)

Answers may vary.

2. We wore great big grins.
3. We cried so much it hurt.
4. Our classroom belongs in Ripley's Believe It or Not.

Editor in Chief (page 211)

trofee, trofe → trophy
congragelated → congratulated
blury → blurry

Topic Sentences (page 212)

page 61   Zev's Deli / one of my favorite places to go
page 62   living with a little brother / can be hard
page 63   our neighborhood / needs sidewalks

Types of Paragraphs (page 212)

1. b   2. a   3. d   4. c

The Forms of Writing

Five-Part Harmony (page 217)

1. heading
2. salutation
3. body
4. closing
5. signature

Knowing Your A's and B's (page 218)

Answers will vary.

Belgium
Canada
Dominican Republic
Egypt

Words About Books (page 219)

2. is an invented or made-up story.
3. is the action in a story.
4. is the time and place of a story.

And the Envelope, Please (page 220)

THE PRESIDENT OF THE UNITED STATES
THE WHITE HOUSE
1600 PENNSYLVANIA AVE
WASHINGTON DC 20500

The Tools of Learning

Just the Right Word (page 226)

Possible synonyms: sprint, jog, dash, bound, gallop, trot

First Cousins (page 226)

Possible word relatives: rainbow, raincoat, rainfall, rainstorm, rainy, rained

Proofreader's Guide

Don't forget contractions! (page 230)

1. you're
2. don't
3. it's
5. they're
6. isn't
7. wasn't

The Poem "True Blue" (page 231)

1. "Elephant Poem"
2. "No Homework"
3. "When I Grow Up"

Spelling It Out (page 231)

1. RAN
2. PAWS
3. HELP
4. NATO
5. CARE
6. MADD
7. NASA

Words or Numerals? (page 231)

1. words
2. words
3. numerals
4. numerals, words
5. numerals
6. numerals

Mail from AL to WY (page 232)

1. TX
2. NY
3. FL
4. UT
5. MI
6. CA
7. DC
8. WV
9. KS
10. IN
11. CT
12. MS

Hidden Names (page 232)

1. Lee
2. Gus
3. Earl
4. Al
5. Marc
6. Rob
7. Ed
8. Ward
9. April
10. Bea
11. Bette
12. Ember
13. Jan
14. Jo
15. May
16. Ruth

The Other Half (page 233)

1. ant
2. wood
3. deer
4. new
5. no
6. peace
7. passed
8. threw
9. there, they're
10. your

Rhyming Lists (page 233)

caught	right
bought	fight
fought	might
taught	sight
thought	tonight

"I won another one!" (page 234)

2. one
3. won
4. one
5. one
6. won

Calling All Nouns (page 236)

1. notes
2. messages
3. letters
4. envelope
5. stamp
6. note
7. person
8. fun
9. note

For the Birds (page 236)

we, I, you, I, you, I, you, me

It will . . . (page 237)

It will snow a lot tomorrow, so school will let out early. It will start to snow before lunch. At first, a few big flakes will come floating down. Then it will come down harder and harder. Snow will pile up on the playground. At 12:30, the principal will announce that school will let out at 1:00. Thanks to the snowstorm, we will have a free afternoon!

Quickly or Slowly? (page 237)

Answers may vary.

Preposition Mission (page 237)

(out of) the school's front door
(at) the traffic light
(to) Moffit's Market
(on) the corner
(on) the right

Student Almanac

Greetings! (page 238)

1. dzău
2. bonjour
3. salaam
4. hola
5. adiós
6. adjö

The Geese and Swans of Puddle Lake (page 239)

duck: drake, duckling, brace/herd
goose: gander, gosling, flock/gaggle
swan: cob, pen, cygnet, bevy/flock

Cups, Pints, Quarts (page 240)

1. 1 2. 2 3. 1 4. 8 5. 4

Silly Millimeter (page 240)

2. centimeter
3. meter
4. kilometer
5. meters

X + Y = 17 (page 241)

$7 + 10 = 17$ $9 + 8 = 17$
$8 + 9 = 17$ $10 + 7 = 17$

Challenge answer: 11

Rounding to the Nearest 10 (page 241)

50, 120, 10, 210, 100

Digital Clocks (page 242)

1. 1:11, 2:22, 3:33, 4:44, 5:55, 11:11
2. 7:07, 7:27, 7:37, 7:47, 7:57
3. 9:11
4. 1:35, 2:46, 3:57, and backward 7:53, 6:42, 5:31

Sharing Borders (page 242)

1. Alaska, Hawaii
2. Maine
3. Rhode Island, South Carolina, Florida, Washington
4. Tennessee

Capital Idea! (page 242)

Dover, Delaware
Honolulu, Hawaii
Indianapolis, Indiana
Oklahoma City, Oklahoma

Name That State (page 243)

1. Texas
2. Idaho
3. New Jersey
4. Illinois

Birds, Beasts, Or? (page 243)

1. Alabama, Louisiana
2. Michigan, Oregon, Wisconsin
3. Utah

Challenge answer: ME, CT, GA, MS, SC, WA, OH

Traveling Through History (page 243)

1. Robert Fulton, 1802
2. Kirkpatrick Macmillan, 1839
3. Charles and Frank Duryea, 1893
4. Orville and Wilbur Wright, 1903

The Start of Something Good (page 244)

1. popcorn   1630
2. hot dogs   1900
3. potato chips 1925
4. ice cream   1786
5. root beer   1866

Index

A

B

C

D

E

F

✱ The start-up and enrichment activities are found after each set of chapter notes.